SUMMIT

PROMOTIONAL PRODUCTS SUCCESS

SUMMIT

REACHING THE PEAK OF YOUR POTENTIAL

Paul A Kiewiet MAS+

Copyright ©2021 by Paul A Kiewiet. All rights reserved. No portion of this book may be reproduced mechanically, electronically, or by any other means, including but not limited to photocopying, recording, scanning, digitizing, taping, web distribution, information networks, information storage or retrieval systems, except as permitted by Section 107 or 108 of the 1976 Copyright Act, without prior written permission of the publisher.

Published by Paul A Kiewiet MAS+
Grand Rapids, MI

ISBN: 9798579244932
1 Business. 2. Marketing 3. Promotion. 4. Promotional Products.

First Printing 2021
Printed in the United States of America

This book is dedicated to my wife,
April Chernoby
who has inspired and challenged me in my sixth and seventh decades of life to reach for new heights, learn new skills and dare new challenges.

TABLE OF CONTENTS

FOREWORD 1

PREFACE 3

INTRODUCTION 7

CHAPTER 1
Ten Things You Need To Know To Become A Promotional Professional. ... 13

CHAPTER 2
Nine Ways to Build Your Personal Brand 15

CHAPTER 3
8 Questions to Ask Every Client 19

CHAPTER 4
7 Ways to start a relationship with a new customer. 23

CHAPTER 5
6 Clients You Need to Fire NOW! 27

CHAPTER 6
5 Questions You Must Answer to Make This Your Best Year Ever 31

CHAPTER 7
The 4 P's of Success 35

CHAPTER 8
Get Curious About Your Business (Ask "Why?" Three Times) 37

CHAPTER 9
Two Ways to Find Your Why? 39

CHAPTER 10
This One Thing. Create. 43

CHAPTER 11
POSITIVITY • ASK • INSPIRE • NEGOTIATE (The First Four Steps to PAIN RELIEF) 47

CHAPTER 12
REINVENT (The next step to PAIN RELIEF) 51

CHAPTER 13
EVALUATE • LIVE • INNOVATE (three more steps to PAIN RELIEF) 55

CHAPTER 14
ENDURE • FUTURE (the final two steps to PAIN RELIEF 59

CHAPTER 15
Seize the Opportunity 63

CHAPTER 16
Are You Ready for Good Things to Happen? 65

CHAPTER 17
What New Skills will you Need to Succeed in the New Economy? 69

CHAPTER 18
Lessons From "The Great One" 73

CHAPTER 19
Scary Stuff— Innovate or Die 75

CHAPTER 20
When Will You Start? 77

CHAPTER 21
The Success Habits in the Age of COVID-19 81

CHAPTER 22
They're still buying, if you offer what they're looking for... 83

CHAPTER 23
Things Are Changing. Whether for the Good or the Bad is Your Decision. 87

CHAPTER 24
5 Mindset Adjustments You Need to Make Now! 91

CHAPTER 25
COVID-19. This too is a Defining Moment 93

CHAPTER 26
Find Your FOCUS 97

CHAPTER 27
Quit Trying to Be Everything to Everyone. 99

CHAPTER 28
Are You Better Than You Were Yesterday? 101

CHAPTER 29
If you don't know, how will they know? 103

CHAPTER 30
To Increase Your Sales—Quit Selling 105

CHAPTER 31
How Are You Different? 109

CHAPTER 32
What Problem Do You Solve? 111

CHAPTER 33
Create A Brand YOU! 113

CHAPTER 34
5 Smart Ways to Grow Your Business 115

CHAPTER 35
Take it to the next level. 117

CHAPTER 36
Why Should They Choose You? 119

CHAPTER 37
How Did You Become A Commodity? 123

CHAPTER 38
The ONLY Marketing You Need 125

CHAPTER 39
Before and After 127

CHAPTER 40
But HOW Can You Be Different 129

CHAPTER 41
It is Not Your Customer's Job to Remember You 133

CHAPTER 42
Do you CARE Enough? 135

CHAPTER 43
Each Moment is a Defining Moment 137

CHAPTER 44
Mindful Prospecting 139

CHAPTER 45
The Secrets of Prospecting 141

CHAPTER 46
Could This Be LOVE? 145

CHAPTER 47
They Want to Love You 147

CHAPTER 48
Get the Job! 149

CHAPTER 49
Get Real 151

CHAPTER 50
Know Your Customer 153

CHAPTER 51
Wishing and Hoping Will Not Take You to the Summit 157

CHAPTER 52
Build Up the Basics 159

CHAPTER 53
Choose Your Mountain 163

CHAPTER 54
Choose Your Route 167

CHAPTER 55
Find Your Community 169

CHAPTER 56
Get A Good Guide 171

CHAPTER 57
Have the Right Gear—and Know How to Use It! 175

CHAPTER 58
Plan, Plan, Plan. And Plan Some More. 179

CHAPTER 59
It Won't Be Easy. Do It Anyway. 181

CHAPTER 60
Success is a Mental Game 183

ABOUT THE AUTHOR 185

FOREWORD

It was his written words that first made me notice Paul Kiewiet. I had recently joined PPAI and a letter to the editor in an industry publication articulating the roles of our association and other industry players struck me as incredibly insightful. I called Paul to congratulate him on the letter and we began a professional friendship that has grown over the past twenty years.

He came to our industry with a background in point of purchase displays. When his clients were concerned about getting their displays put up at retail, he discovered the Premium Incentive Industry where he became a volunteer, speaker and leader in incentive associations.

It was at one of those meetings where he met PPAI Hall of Fame member, Glen Holt who encouraged him to discover the promotional products industry.

It wasn't long before he was volunteering, serving on committees, speaking and writing about things like "need creation" vs "need fulfillment" and how to be a marketer rather than an order taker. Professionally, he was growing his distributorship—he called it a sales promotion agency—into a multimillion-dollar firm building national brands.

When he was elected to the PPAI Board of Directors in 2004, I came to appreciate his passion for teaching practitioners to treat the industry as a profession. Over the years, he's been a prolific writer on not selling products but on diagnosing client problems and using promotional products as what he often calls, "the aspirin."

As the chairman of the board of PPAI in 2007-2008, he pushed hard for product safety and responsibility throughout the supply chain. Forming a Global Strategy Council, he made two trips to China to bring the message to manufacturers over there. He was a Trustee for PPAI with the Forum for People Performance Management and Measurement and spoke on the importance of people in marketing and brand-building. He also pushed for greater involvement in the larger Advertising Industry recommending our initial involvement in Advertising Week in New York City where he was a featured speaker for our first three years there.

As chairman, his monthly column in PPB won an Excel Award from a magazine publishers' group. A five-part series on how to sell promotional products as an advertising medium for our magazine won the prestigious Folio Award.

In *Summit: Reaching the Peak of Your Potential*, he has compiled a "best of" from a career of sharing his unique vision of using the promotional products industry as a vehicle for personal and professional growth and of service to others. Kiewiet references a failed attempt to summit Mt. Ararat in Turkey but goes on to explain how the lessons learned by pushing his comfort zone has led him to even greater heights to the top of Mt. Kilimanjaro.

I knew Paul when his world came crashing down. I also witnessed resilience in practice. The lessons he shares in this book are personal to him, but also universal for all of us. I hope you find inspiration, motivation and personal growth from his words.

This book is a guide for anyone who wants to move their business away from selling commodities and become a value creator. Paul has always had a clear view of what promotional products can do. In this book, he shares how to become a problem-solving artist and climb to their own peak of success.

PAUL BELLANTONE CAE
former President and CEO
PPAI
Dallas, TX
April 2021

PREFACE

THE THUNDER BLIZZARD finally quieted. Tucked in a sleeping bag fourteen thousand feet above sea level on the legendary Mt Ararat trying to get a couple hours of shut eye before starting out for the summit in the early morning hours. Heavy winds had buffeted the tiny tent and made us worry about being crushed by the huge boulders surrounding us. This was my first attempt to summit a legendary peak.

Mount Ararat is located in extreme eastern Turkey near the border with Armenia and just ten miles from Iran. A dormant volcano, the 16,854 ft snow-capped summit makes it the highest point in Turkey and the third most prominent mountain in West Asia. According to the Biblical account, Noah's ark came to rest "on the mountains of Ararat" which has made searches for the ark on this mountain an explorer's obsession. Our 2013 ascent was strictly for adventure, but one of the most frequently asked question I've gotten has been, "Did you find Noah's Ark?" And my favorite reply—"No, but we did see his dinghy."

The summit was a worthy goal. The first day hike started at about a 5000 feet above sea level passing pastoral scenes of nomadic families and young herders tending their flocks. As we passed 10,000 ft to Green Camp, the air was noticeably thinner and the footsteps shorter. The second day seemed cruel. It was "acclimation" day to get acclimated to the higher altitude. We hiked all day to High Camp at 14,000 feet only to turn around and return to Green Camp. That night we experienced our first thunderstorm on the mountain that felt like we had awakened a beast that would throw us off its back. The next morning, we packed up and again hiked to High Camp. The glacier surrounded High Camp and the summit day to follow would require crampons and ice axes to reach the summit.

Ignoring advice from my wife, I put my crampons on for the first time. Ever! The previous winter April had encouraged me to try them out in our Michigan winter, but I had demurred. To me it seemed one is just walking with spikes on their boots. During my trial on the glacier, my right crampon broke under my weight. We rigged it up and crossed our fingers. After dinner we went to our tent early but soon the storm came and dumped fresh snow on the mountain top.

Around midnight, Yosef, our guide went tent to tent to rouse our expedition. The doubts came on strong. Could I make the ascent on one crampon if I needed? What about the ice axe? Was this a good place to learn how to use it? I had fallen a couple of times on the ascent to High Camp. Could I arrest a fall if it happened on the glacier? After breakfast, our group headed out. Our headlamps, the only illumination as we took a step, took a breath and started the final ascent to the summit. With each step, the self-doubts and negative self-talk nagged at me until finally I just stopped. I watched my friends continue the light parade up as I turned around and walked back down to the tent.

This was a place that did not allow for second thoughts. Or third or wavering. There was no way to turn around again and safely try to catch up with the group. There was just me in my tent with my own tortured thoughts. This was a summit that wasn't. It was also an education on how not to reach a summit. I'll share many of those lessons in this book.

I spent my life in the world of marketing—point of purchase merchandising, premium and incentives, sales promotion and promotional products. As an entrepreneur, I founded a successful sales promotion agency / promotional products distributorship and became a recognized expert, speaker, writer and consultant. My "Why" is to inspire and challenge others so that we can discover our full potential. Over the years, I've published thousands of words about how to grow as a professional in industries that have no clear path or roadmap.

I sold my agency several years ago to focus on doing only the things I love doing—helping others grow, helping others discover their mountain and being their guide to reach the summit. That summit is not the same for each person and discovering the right summit is a part of the process as well.

The year following my failure to summit Mt Ararat, I stood at the highest point of the African continent, Mt Kilimanjaro, 19,310 feet above sea level, the highest free-standing mountain and one of the fabled Seven Summits. Summit Day on Kilimanjaro was fifth anniversary of the death of my first wife and mother of my children on the day of my mother's funeral after a year in which life threw everything it could at me.

Life has a way of testing us. Just as summiting a great peak does. These are journeys of discovery. Five months after the summit of Kilimanjaro, I was diagnosed and had a malignant tumor removed from my colon. And less than one month after that surgery, I stood in front of a crowd of professional colleagues and received induction into the Promotional Products Association International's Hall of Fame.

In this book, I'll share many of the lessons I've learned as I've attempted and summited my way through a life in the promotion industry.

The day my gastroenterologist informed me that the biopsy had come back and used the "C" word, was the full experience of surreal. It was the first time I really stared at my own mortality. There was the ambiguousness of not knowing. What stage was the cancer? Would I need chemotherapy? Radiation? Would I need a colostomy? Would I be given an expiration date?

Strangely, one of my thoughts on that afternoon was that I never got around to writing a book. Despite hundreds of articles, blogs, speeches, presentations and the occasional urging of friends to publish—I never made the time. Yet somehow, I still waited another five years before making the decision to summit that peak.

This book is a compilation of a decade of writing and of my favorite articles, tips and thoughts about how to become a leader in the amazing world of promotional marketing. Most of the ideas are universal and can be applied across industries and are applicable to your personal side as well.

INTRODUCTION

"Never waste a good crisis". I've heard this from former PPAI President Paul Bellantone and it's one of those great phrases that you may not be sure you understand if it applies, but somehow, it just feels right. I guess this book may be my way of honoring that thought.

Everyone has been affected by the Great Pandemic of 2020-2021. For most of us, business is anywhere from down to devastated. Change in so many areas of our lives has accelerated. More of our clients are working from home. Events, which drive more than 40% of our industry sales have moved to virtual or been canceled completely. Many people who were not fans of buying online, now do nearly all of their research and buying from a device.

"This too shall pass"—once a reassuring, Zen-like comfort is not a promise. Yes, the pandemic will pass. The economy will bounce back. But how we reach our customers, how we grow relationships has some permanent alterations. Some companies will continue with work from home policies making your buyers harder to meet. Many of us will need to really improve our online presence, build ecommerce capabilities to match the competition and have a real social media game. Some clients of certain ages may decide to retire. Your new buyers may be younger, think differently, look differently and make buying decisions differently.

When I decided to put together this compilation of my writings, I was struck by just how applicable the advice written during some of my earlier life crises are today. Some things are timeless.

It has been said that adversity builds character. My experience with life is that it reveals character. In the midst of all of these changes, some things do stay the same. Who you are and the values you live by can be your constant—your guide star—to bring you through these challenging times. Throughout this book you will have several reminders of the absolute power there is in passion and living out your values.

There is never a better time than the present to reinvent yourself, your business and your skills. Now is that time. You will never have more opportunity to grow than right now. Because right now is all there really is. Now is your opportunity to grow. Grow as a person. Grow your business. Grow your network.

Success means different things to different people. *Summit: Reaching the Peak of Your Potential* defines success as constantly stretching yourself to discover your full potential. It means knowing your purpose and living it. That means you will be forced to the edges of your comfort zone. It is at those edges where you find the good stuff that will deliver your answer about what your life is about.

To summit the peak of your potential you need to RISE. This requires...

Resilience:

> Successful people get knocked down. The reason they are a success is that they get back up. History is filled with our heroes who met life's challenges and disappointments with resolve and got back up time and time again. Abraham Lincoln famously failed several times before being elected the 16TH President of the United States and saving the Union.

> Life can knock us down from no fault of our own. Great Recessions can occur. International pandemics can arrive. Great clients can go bankrupt or suddenly be acquired, moved or have personnel changes that leave your sales devastated. Personal losses can come—sickness, divorce, death. We can do everything right and life will simply mock us and show us that it has the final say in the rules of the game.

Inspire:

> Be your own inspiration. The origin of the word is to be "in spirit". My personal "why" statement—"to challenge and inspire others so that we can reach our full potential" points to how to get yourself inspired. Do so by inspiring others. Be a positive force in your world. Encourage others and help them grow.

> Inspiration will also work your creativity muscles. Writers, musicians,

artists and dancers are thought of as inspired as they express their art. I believe that promotional professionals are also artists as we solve problems, build brands and stir the emotions of clients and their customers.

STRATEGIC:

To write your own story and summit your own peaks, you need to have a vision of what you want your life to look like. You need to know which mountains you want to climb. This requires that you think through the how to create the life you desire and the to get the results you are looking for.

Strategy means planning under conditions of uncertainty. It is that uncertainty that prompted Dwight D. Eisenhower to say, "Plans are worthless, but planning is everything." Being strategic means you think about when you may need to zig and when you may need to zag. You are intentional, yet flexible.

EXCELLENCE:

Being good is the cost of entry, the baseline. Strive every day to excellence. Throughout this book—there is a who section dedicated to it—the importance of differentiation is highlighted. Nobody notices good. Average is just the best of the worst or the worst of the best.

Face it. Selling promotional products can mean selling the same stuff from the same suppliers to the same buyers in the same way as your competitors. You need to add extra value to move from good to excellent. Stan Phelps speaks about this in *Purple Goldfish: Little Things Make the Biggest Difference* suggesting that we add "marketing lagniappe"—a Cajun concept of adding a little bit more in every transaction.

Deliver those four values and you will RISE above the competition and rise up to the summit of your potential.

I've divided *Summit: Reaching the Peak of Your Potential* into six parts. Most of the chapters are brief, thought-provoking and bite-size. Many of the chapters in this book began life as blog posts intended as daily inspiration.

Part 1 is Countdown to Success which is a series in which each chapter enumerates in descending order from Ten Ways to Be a Professional down to This One Thing. In Part 2 ten chapters spell out PAIN RELIEF which is our recipe to Thrive in Any Economy. Part 3 delivers ten Success Strategies You Need Now. Part 4 gives you ten chapters on how you can Differentiate yourself from your competition. Part 5 is about the inside job you need to do on yourself to experience Success from The Inside Out.

Summit closes with Part 6. All new material on the lessons from climbing real mountains and how you can apply them to your life and your business to reach the peak of your potential.

Thank you for being my climbing partner and allowing me to be your guide on this journey.

PAUL A. KIEWIET MAS+
Grand Rapids, MI
February 2021

SUMMIT
REACHING THE PEAK OF YOUR POTENTIAL

Part 1: Countdown To Success

CHAPTER 1: TEN THINGS YOU NEED TO KNOW TO BECOME A PROMOTIONAL PROFESSIONAL

CHAPTER 2: NINE WAYS TO BUILD YOUR PERSONAL BRAND

CHAPTER 3: EIGHT QUESTIONS TO ASK EVERY CLIENT

CHAPTER 4: SEVEN WAYS TO START A RELATIONSHIP WITH A NEW CLIENT

CHAPTER 5: SIX CLIENTS YOU NEED TO FIRE NOW!

CHAPTER 6: FIVE QUESTIONS YOU MUST ANSWER TO MAKE THIS YOUR BEST YEAR EVER

CHAPTER 7: THE 4 P'S OF SUCCESS

CHAPTER 8: GET CURIOUS ABOUT YOUR BUSINESS (ASK "WHY?" THREE TIMES)

CHAPTER 9: TWO WAYS TO FIND YOUR "WHY?"

CHAPTER 10: THIS ONE THING. CREATE

10 THINGS YOU NEED TO KNOW

To become a promotional professional

 1. WORK WITH A COACH.

2. ASSOCIATE WITH GOOD PEOPLE.

 3. WORK ON WHO YOU ARE.

4. DON'T RUSH TO MAKE A SALE.

 5. BE A STUDENT OF THE INDUSTRY.

6. DON'T LET IT DRIVE YOU CRAZY.

 7. NEVER COMPETE ON PRICE.

8. DON'T TRY TO DO IT ALL.

 9. HAVE A PASSION!

10. HAVE FUN!

TEN THINGS YOU NEED TO DO TO BECOME A PROMOTIONAL PROFESSIONAL.

CHAPTER 1
TEN THINGS YOU NEED TO KNOW TO BECOME A PROMOTIONAL PROFESSIONAL.

1. All major sports teams have coaches. If you want to play in the major league, get coaching. Our industry has several good ones.

2. If you want to be good, hang around those who already are. Your regional association is where the really good hang out. Get involved, volunteer, serve. You'll meet the best in the industry. You'll find your mentor.

3. Customers remember only a few of your words. They never forget the essence of who you are. Work on who you are, more than what you say.

4. Don't rush to make a sale. Clients forgive a lot of the things that can go wrong with an order. A bad recommendation, a promotion that makes them look bad is forever.

5. Everything you ever wanted to know about promotional products can be learned at your regional and international associations. Read the publications from cover to cover. Attend every workshop, seminar and presentation that you can. You are lucky to be in an industry with the breadth of free education and professional development it offers.

6. This is a crazy business, but that doesn't mean that you need to go crazy. Don't go bonkers if someone drops the ball sometimes. It's going to happen. I know of no long-term calamities befalling mankind because of a screwed-up order. Yes, it is the end of the world. Until you let go, take the lessons from it and move on.

7. Never compete on price. No one wins.

8. Don't try to do it all. Everything you learn from reps, from PPAI, from ASI, from your regionals, from your reps shouldn't be everything you do. Take only what fits for you, your style, your market, and leave the rest behind.

9. Have a passion for what you do. It will help you get through those missed deadlines, lost packages, bad artwork, unrealistic clients, unreliable resources and those days when the entire universe conspires against you.

10. Have fun. If you are not enjoying what you are doing, why do it?

9 WAYS TO BUILD YOUR PERSONAL BRAND

1. ESTABLISH EXPECTATIONS

2. MAKE IT MEMORABLE

3. TELL STORIES

4. BE A FRIEND

5. KNOW WHAT YOU STAND FOR

6. KNOW WHAT YOU'RE GOOD AT AND BE GREAT AT IT

7. BE CONSISTENT

8. MAKE YOUR MARK

9. PROMOTE YOUR BRAND

CHAPTER 2
NINE WAYS TO BUILD YOUR PERSONAL BRAND

You are a Brand. Your brand is you and you take it with you wherever you go, whether you work for yourself or for someone else. It even follows you if you change industries. But here's the thing, Brand YOU is constantly evolving and you can continuously build your brand.

My favorite definition of brand comes from one of my favorite business thinkers and writers, Seth Godin. I've modified it just a bit to relate to your personal brand as a promotional professional. "A brand is the set of expectations, memories, stories and relationships that, taken together, account for a client's decision to choose one provider over another. If the buyer doesn't pay a premium, make a selection or spread the word, then no brand value exists for that buyer. Your brand's value is merely the sum total of how much extra people will pay, or how often they choose the expectations, memories, stories and relationships of one brand over the alternatives."

So how do you go about building your personal brand? Here are nine suggestions:

1. Establish expectations for remarkable experiences.

You must always be stretching beyond good. Never be satisfied with delivering a good product at a good price on time. Everyone who is still is business does those things. Those are the cost of entry into the game. With every interaction with your customers, you need to leave them feeling great about themselves and about you. Set a standard for yourself to be fascinating, remarkable, outstanding. Create high expectations for yourself and then deliver.

2. Make it memorable.

What are the little extras that you can do to make your interactions with your clients memorable? Your customer will remember the handwritten thank you note that your send. She'll remember the extra spec samples that you had made up to show her what her logo would look like on some additional ways to help her achieve her goals. He'll remember that you took the time to provide a post-project review of what worked, what could be better and the results of the program. They'll even remember that your invoice was accurate, timely and conformed to their corporate requirements. Your brand is built with the details and the extras.

3. Tell Stories.

People love stories. Tell them. From earliest childhood and going back through history, it is the story tellers who become leaders. How can you reframe your presentations into stories? Use case histories. Ask your reps about successful uses and applications. Make the stories personal, funny, compelling and you'll gain a reputation of someone who understands his business.

4. Be a friend.

Always make it about the relationship. Get to know your customers and you'll learn what is important to them. You will just naturally be looking out for their best interest. You will take the Golden Rule and move it up a notch to the Platinum Rule: Do Unto Others As They Would Have Done For Them. Friends do favors without keeping score. Friends genuinely like each other. Friends have something to talk about even if there isn't an immediate business project at stake.

5. Know What You Stand For and Take a Stand.

If your brand is to be known for something, you need to define it. Choose honesty, integrity, reliability, of course. But go deeper. What is it that you stand for and then be uncompromising on your principles. Become known as being impeccable. If you know what you are worth, charge for it and never lower your price without taking something back in return.

6. Know What You're Good At and Be Great At it.

A specialist in any profession makes more money and is in higher demand than any generalist. With the hundreds of thousands of products and hundreds of categories available in our industry, you simply cannot be the best at all of them. Choose your niche, choose your product category, choose your client industry and then work at becoming world-class at them. It will mean sometimes saying "no" to a tempting client or project. Define yourself and become the favorite brand in your category.

7. Be Consistent.

Brands are built over time. Being consistent means that you follow your principles always. It means that you are authentic and transparent. It means that you remind yourself every single day of who you are, why you are doing what you are doing, and you provide value. Every single day you need to be turning strangers into friends, friends into customers and those customers into raving fans.

8. Make Your Mark.

Get serious about becoming a brand. Buy a domain name that is uniquely you. It can be your name, your nickname, your brand name, even what you do. If you have a unique name, make that your brand name. Or create a combination of your name and your specialty. You may even create a logo for yourself. But your mark can be your colors, your apparel, your briefcase, your scent, sound or any of the senses. Just as major brands change and update their logos, you can as well. Be noticeable and be noticeably consistent.

9. Promote Your Brand.

You're in the advertising, marketing and promotion business. You must promote. Promote your brand by providing useful content—like a friend would—free. Use your social media presence to extend your reach, but make sure you are following the previous principles in all of your promotion. Be yourself and be true to yourself.

Work constantly on becoming the preferred brand in your category. Build it and they will become raving fans!

FIND the *Pain*

BE the *Aspirin*

CHAPTER 3
8 QUESTIONS TO ASK EVERY CLIENT

If you want better answers, ask better questions. It is impossible to serve your clients and create value for them unless you have a thorough understanding of their organization. Information gathering should be personal, conversational, tailored to the person you are speaking with in the moment. When and how you ask should also be based on how well-known the company is, the position of the person you are meeting with and how much pre-approach research you have done. I recommend that you use the internet, the library, LinkedIn and other sources to gather information before your meeting. Some of these questions you may already know the answer to, and you will be able to impress the prospect with your diligence.

1. What is your primary mission? Try to find out why they are in business. The why will determine the what. Let me explain. If you called on Apple with the presumption that they were in the computer business, you wouldn't ask the right questions or get the right answers. Larger companies will have their mission statement posted on their website, in their annual report, perhaps even hanging in their lobby. Pay attention to the words that they use and incorporate those words into your language.

2. How do you go to market? Find out how they reach their final end buyer. They may sell through multiple channel partners such as distributors who in turn sell to dealers who in turn sell to the ultimate consumer. Some may have brick and mortar stores and others an online presence and still others a combination.

3. What is the most unique characteristic of your company? Try to determine what makes them distinctive. How are they different from their competitors? Which leads to...

4. Who are your competitors? Find out how they rank in their product or service category. Are they the market leader, a new player on the field, a follower? Armed with this information, you can find out what their competitors are doing well and where they may be vulnerable.

5. What trade shows do you attend? Which trade shows do you exhibit at? What trade publications do you subscribe to? With this information, you can take several business building steps. You can subscribe to their trade publications which will give you a feel for what their industry problems, challenges and trends are looking like and give you more information about the prospect and their competitors. It may also give you the opportunity attend one of their industry trade shows where again, you get a big picture perspective on their industry as well as pick up additional leads for potential clients. And, of course, it allows you to write down the names and dates of the shows that they will be exhibiting at so that you can prepare a proposal for them AFTER you know why and what you should be suggesting.

6. What is the biggest business challenge facing you right now? You want to find out where their pain is. Are they losing market share? Facing dwindling consumer loyalty? Growing too fast? Need to find new markets? Has the internet and technology shifts helped them or hurt them? You need to find the pain and be the aspirin. Listen carefully for how they characterize their problems.

7. What does success look like? What are your objectives? How will things look when they are accomplished? How do you want people to feel about your organization? What is getting

in the way from accomplishing these goals? What resources are needed to reach them?

8. What was your greatest (sales, marketing, advertising, human resources, public relations—you choose which one or ones you want to ask about—success? And what was the worst? You want to find out what has worked and what has not worked. If possible, you want to find out if there was a bad promotional product experience. Knowing what the client felt was the greatest will give you an idea of what they look for in a successful promotion. Knowing what they think is the worst might prevent you from walking in with a proposal that has zero chance of being accepted.

When you ask better questions, you get to know where you can be looking for opportunities. You can proactively recommend programs and solutions aimed at their particular problems. When a client sees that you are focused on solving their problems, that you have put some good thinking into their challenges and that you provide solid marketing advice, they see a professional. You will find that even if your proposal is not quite ready for prime time, that they will respect how you think and will open up even more with you about what they are working on and what projects are in the pipeline.

For better answers, ask better questions.

7 WAYS TO START A RELATIONSHIP WITH A NEW CUSTOMER

1. GET TO KNOW THEM. BEFORE YOU MEET THEM.

2. MAKE THEIR LIFE BETTER

3. KEEP IT REAL

4. CREATE VALUE

5. BE A STORY STELLER

6. MAKE IT EASY TO WORK TOGETHER

7. DON'T TAKE ANYTHING PERSONALLY

"The most profitable clients are built through the hard work of getting to know them, to understanding their motivations and their problems and coming up with solutions that are totally framed around them."

CHAPTER 4
7 WAYS TO START A RELATIONSHIP WITH A NEW CUSTOMER.

In order to develop relationships with new prospects and turn those strangers into friends, you need to work at it and be real. This requires that you take the necessary steps that will help you gain trust and turn those friends into customers. Here are seven tips that can help you with that.

1. **Get to know them.**

    You need to learn everything you can about the prospect as a person and their company. Spend the time to check both the person and the company out online. Check them out on Google, LinkedIn, Facebook, Twitter, Pinterest. Get to know them. From the company's online presence, you should be able to pick up on the words they use, their mission, vision and the image they are trying to project.

    Try to get a sense of their beliefs and how they align with your own. Who are they and what do you have in common? What are their feelings about your message?

2. **How will you make their life better?**

    It is all about them. If you can't make their life better, why are you calling on them? What is the result you will deliver for them? Most likely they want more money, more sales, more customers, more profits and less work and less stress. But don't assume. Get very clear on your promise. Until you can get very clear and articulate the transformation that you can offer them, you're not ready to call on them.

3. **KEEP IT REAL.**

    Assuming that you are a good person with ethics and who really cares about other people, be that person. There is no place for old school manipulation, pressure or guilting in building relationships. You should be able to feel good about what you're about to ask for and the recommendations that you are making. Your new friend should also feel like it is the natural next step. People can spot a phony or a sleaze a mile away. Don't be a phony or a sleaze.

4. **CREATE VALUE.**

    Don't you hate this cliche? It's not. It's the hard work, the counter-intuitive work that you need to be doing. How do you create value? You do it by giving away ideas. You do it by sharing ideas and best practices. When you leave your customer after a meeting, are they better off than when you showed up? Do they have something that they feel good about or that they can implement now? Have you left them wanting more? What's the best tip you can share with them today that is going to make their life better now?

5. **BE A STORYTELLER.**

    Take them to a place with you where their problems go away. Learn how to tell stories. Stories engage both the brain and the heart and gives you an emotional connection. Stories allow them to get into the movie you are creating, and it allows imagination to move them along with you. There is something primal about a story. Become a talented storyteller and they will always want to hear more from you.

6. **MAKE IT EASY TO WORK TOGETHER.**

    Consider from the other's point of view what obstacles there might be for you working together. Remove them ahead of time. Don't make it confusing, don't put in a lot of conditions. Lay it all out and tell them what the next steps are, how you will work for them, how you will keep them informed and how you will make them look good. Find out if they want you to bundle all of the extra costs such as set-up charges and freight. Be aware of the processes that they need to follow and put together a proposal that already anticipates their processes. Be very clear and very easy to work with and make it very easy for them to justify working with you.

7. **DON'T TAKE ANYTHING PERSONALLY.**

    Sometimes you won't get your way. If you created a solution that you believe in and they didn't buy, feel good about yourself. Sometimes it works out, sometimes it doesn't. If you are desperate to make a sale, it will be obvious and it will be an obvious turn-off. Create something great, offer it to them and then let go of the decision. You want to feel good about your work and you want to leave the door open to try again.

The most profitable clients are built through the hard work of getting to know them, to understanding their motivations and their problems and coming up with solutions that are totally framed around them. It's a form of servant leadership. When you serve their needs, you earn their trust. When you earn their trust, you develop loyal customers who very often become your biggest fans.

6 CLIENTS TO FIRE NOW!

1. "I'LL GLADLY PAY YOU TUESDAY FOR A HAMBURGER TODAY" (ALWAYS ASKING FOR FAVORS WITHOUT PAYBACK)

2. THEY WON'T PAY YOU ON TIME

3. "THANKS FOR THE IDEAS, THE SAMPLES, THE DESIGN. NOW I JUST NEED TO SHOP THIS AROUND."

4. THEY MAKE YOU UNCOMFORTABLE

5. THEY ARE DISRESPECTFUL

6. THEY DON'T LET YOU MAKE A FAIR PROFIT.

"Focus on your great clients and grow within their companies. Remember why you're in business."

CHAPTER 5
6 CLIENTS YOU NEED TO FIRE NOW!

Many of us hold the mistaken belief that the more clients we have the more money we make. That is a myth that does not serve us well. My first great breakthrough on my quest to become a multimillion-dollar producer was that to get to the next level, I needed to fire the deadwood out of my client list. The first year that I did this, I was finally able to break into the seven-figure territory. Pruning the client list allows you to provide better serve your good accounts and to fully realize their potential. It also allows you to be filling your prospect pipeline with more good prospects and do a better job of getting into the types of clients that you want. Here are some of the clients you might want to fire.

"I'll gladly pay you Tuesday for a hamburger today" OK, I realize probably nobody under 40 years old understands that reference to a Popeye character (Google it and find some YouTube videos if you don't understand the reference). Usually, they were the big clients but there were people who were constantly asking for no-profit or at-a-loss favors from me today with the promise of the big order tomorrow. Guess what, tomorrow never comes. If your client is unwilling to allow you to charge a fair price for even the smallest order or favor, let them go. Fire them.

They won't pay you on time. If your customers won't pay you within your terms, they have broken the contract. Let them go. You have a responsibility to your suppliers to pay them according to terms. You have to pay your employees every pay day. Payment terms are called terms because they are the basis of your agreement. If you agree to longer terms than the traditional 30 days, that is your business. But if your terms are net 60 or net 90 and the client is still not paying within those terms—fire them.

"Thanks for the recommendation and the six samples and the design, I think we've figured out what we want now, so I'll just have to get a couple other quotes from other agencies." First of all, shame on you for not making it clear that your research, your artist and your samples do not come free. Include a statement on every quote or proposal that you own the ideas and designs that you submit and that services such as samples and freight for them will be billed if the client chooses to source elsewhere. Base your hourly rate on what your overhead is and quote it. State clearly that your price includes all of your development charges. The first time they do this to you send them an invoice for your time and charges. The second time or the first time they don't pay you for your work—fire them.

You feel your stomach tie into knots every time they call, or you call on them. Just so I'm not crude, I'll need to alter the wording of one of my longstanding principles—" Life is too short to deal with sphincter muscles". If someone makes you feel uncomfortable because of the way, they treat you and other people. Fire Them!

They do not treat you or your people with respect. You are only a vendor, a necessary evil to them. They withhold information and don't give you enough background in order for you to do the best job possible for them. They won't share their budget and make you guess at what they want, why the want it, when they need it. If they swear at you or an employee or show no respect for your professionalism—Fire them.

They don't let you make a fair profit. I fired a company after they spent more than $2 million dollars with me. They wanted to dictate profit margins, payment terms and wouldn't agree to pay for my creative and project expertise. A good friend of mine also fired an account whose brand name would make most of you salivate. Why? Because they set up everything in their favor. You need to know what you are worth, and you need to know the profitability of each account. If they won't let you make what you are worth—Fire Them.

Focus on your great clients and grow within their companies. Find companies that are listed as "Great Places to Work". In my experience, if they treat their employees well, they will also treat their suppliers well. Remember why you are in this business. Have fun, build relationships and get paid for the value that you create.

There must be 50 ways to fire a client.

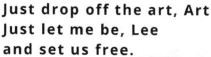

Just drop off the art, Art
Just let me be, Lee
and set us free.

Why fire them?

You deserve respect.
You can use that time profitably.
You get to choose who you work for.

5 QUESTIONS = 1 PLAN

1. What Are You Building?

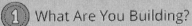

Your Vision

2. Why Are You Building It?

Your Mission

3. What Results Will You Measure?

Your Goals

4. How Will You Build It?

Your Strategies

5. What is the Work To Be Done?

Your Tasks

CHAPTER 6

5 QUESTIONS YOU MUST ANSWER TO MAKE THIS YOUR BEST YEAR EVER

When Alice fell down the rabbit hole, she asked the Cheshire Cat, ""Would you tell me, please, which way I ought to go from here?"

"That depends a good deal on where you want to get to," said the Cat.

"I don't much care where–" said Alice.

"Then it doesn't matter which way you go," said the Cat.

"–so long as I get SOMEWHERE," Alice added as an explanation.

"Oh, you're sure to do that," said the Cat, "if you only walk long enough."

Unfortunately, the vast majority of us are like Alice. We put a lot of effort into going anywhere.

I'm not going to kid you. Reading this article is not going to lead you to success. What will give you a giant leap however is taking the time to really work through each of the five questions that I'm going to pose to you here. These apply to owners, principals, sales managers, salespeople and really anybody. For any part of your life—not just business, but your relationships, your family, your spiritual and personal development. Spend hours forcing yourself to go deep and discover your full potential and your best self.

1. **What Am I Building?**

    If you haven't determined what success looks like, how will you know when you get there? Get very clear on this and be wildly optimistic. Don't limit yourself. Describe your dream. Be passionate and paint a very graphic picture of what you want. Create your possibilities and ask, "what if?" and "why not". The future you deserve is right there for the taking. Grab it.

2. **Why Am I Doing This?**

   Do you know your why? Simon Sinek says, "people don't buy what you do, they buy why you do it." Let me stop you right here. The answer is not "to make money". Making money is a result, not a reason. My personal "why" statement "to inspire and challenge people so that we can reach our full potential."

   Make it short and memorable, communicating your focus and the value you bring to others. It will reflect your driving values and the highest good you can achieve. It may even communicate what it does for your soul.

3. **What Results Will I Measure?**

   As we stand on the doorstep of another new year, think about the celebration dinner you'll host in January of next year. What will you be toasting? Yes, we're talking about your objectives. The purpose of each is to cause you to take meaningful action. Where your answer to the first question is expansive and idealistic, and the answer to the second is short, powerful and customer-focused—your objectives must be designed to focus your resources on achieving specific, measurable, attainable relevant, time-based results (SMART).

   These objectives may be financial, sales-specific, people-oriented, or personal but they must be aligned and relevant to your WHY and your WHAT.

4. **How Will I Build It?**

   Your answers to this will describe how you will be successful over time. They will set the direction, philosophy, values and methodology for building your business or your life. They will be the basis of not just your to-do list but also your "stop doing" list and your "don't even think about it" list.

   Your thought process must go to what you love, what clients you love, what you're best at, what works and how to do more of that. Think also about the opposites and how to do less of it.

You're probably familiar with the SWOT analysis. What are your strengths? Do more of those. What are your weaknesses? Do fewer of those. What opportunities should you be taking advantage of? What are the immediate and future threats to your business? How can you best prepare to meet them and beat them?

5. **WHAT IS THE WORK I NEED TO DO NOW?**

   You know what you're building and why you're building it and what needs to be measured and how you're going to accomplish it. The final question is okay—what do I need to do to take the first steps?

   The plans you create here are the specific actions that must be implemented to achieve the objectives. Each must relate to what you're measuring and how you are going to do it. They must be action-oriented, specific and have deadlines.

   The intent is to keep your focus on the important but not necessarily the urgent tasks. What projects will make a big difference in your business or life? What are the next three steps to make them happen?

You've just created a simple Marketing Plan.

Your answer to Question #1 is your Vision Statement. Why you are building it (#2) is your Mission Statement. You've identified your Objectives (#3) and the Strategies (#4) to make it happen. Now you have the Plans (#5) to make your dreams a reality.

Don't allow yourself to get distracted or sidetracked. Use your plan to guide your decisions and keep you on track all year long. You now know where you are going, how to get there and the steps needed to take you there. So, climb out of your rabbit hole, quit asking Cheshire Cats for directions and follow your path to success starting now.

THE 4 P'S OF SUCCESS

PURPOSE

PASSION

PRINCIPLES

PRACTICES

A purpose-driven, passionate life lived to strong principles and disciplined practices generates the type of trust that facilitates collaboration and meaningful relationships."

CHAPTER 7
THE 4 P'S OF SUCCESS

Since all of us are in marketing, we've all heard of the Four P's—Product, Place, Price and Promotion. However, there are also Four P's to living a successful life.

What brings meaning to your life—you family life, your business life, your inner life? What is the impact you want to have on others and your world? What is the difference you want to make? The answer to this question is your first 'P'—Your **PURPOSE**. Get clear about your purpose and you have a driver of your authenticity.

What do you LOVE to do in not only your personal life and your own time but in your work? What makes you feel alive? What might you do if you could spend your time any way you like? What gets your juices flowing and gives you a sense of joy and accomplishment?

This is your **PASSION**. Your passion brings energy and gives you resilience. It's the booster that keeps you refreshed and enthusiastic for the opportunities in front of you.

What is your guide star? Your north star? What values will direct your decisions and the way you live, work and relate to others? There was a moment in my life when nearly everything around me fell apart and almost everything changed. A friend helped me identify that moment as a defining moment. I could have been consumed by anger and vengeance. At that defining moment, I decided that I was a kind person, and that kindness would be my guiding principle in the tough times, decisions and reactions ahead. What is important to the way you live are your **PRINCIPLES**. Knowing your core values make your decision making easier and provide a light for your path.

What do you do every day to live out your values and accomplish your goals? How do you behave on a daily basis? These are your **PRACTICES** and the fourth of the Four P's of Successful Living. The first three define your self-image and are the core of your personal identity. This fourth one will define your reputation—how other people see and perceive you. When you get all of these aligned, you build trust.

A purpose-driven, passionate life lived to strong principles and disciplined practices generates the type of trust that facilitates collaboration and meaningful relationships. It gives you confidence, clarity and a compass to guide you to and through a successful life journey

ASK 'WHY?' 3 TIMES

WHY?
Why are your customers buying from you right now?

WHY?
Why are your customers staying with you?

WHY?
Why is your competition so successful?

Why is that the why?
and
Why is that the why?
and
Why is that the why?

CHAPTER 8
GET CURIOUS ABOUT YOUR BUSINESS (ASK "WHY?" THREE TIMES)

One of the most valuable practices you can have to build the business you want is to spend some serious thinking time. I don't mean daydreaming. I don't mean just being reflective. I mean getting out a pen and paper or your word processor, maybe Google too and get serious about creating the business that provides both a living and a life.

Like that irritating four-year-old kid, you need to be asking "Why?" and asking it a lot. You need to not only ask it to the point of distraction, but you also need to answer it. Here are three important why questions that you need to find the answers to.

Why are your customers buying from you right now? Do you know the answer to this question? Do you like the answer? Is your answer something that you can replicate and provide to every prospect that you would like to work with? Will your answer still work for you next year? In five years? Can your competition match or become better at your why? Learn and understand what value your customers want and how you can deliver that.

Why are your customers staying with you? Or Why are your customers shopping you? Are your customers constantly pressuring you over price? Do they abandon you to save a few dollars? Do they find value in what you provide? Do they like you personally but view your offerings as purely transactional? How easy would it be for a competitor to replace you? What do you need to do to create loyal customers? Find out what your customers find impressive and amazing so that you can create advocates.

Why is your competition so successful? What is it about their relationship to their customers that makes it that you can't get in the door? What can you learn from them? What do they do that you don't do? Are they selling at a higher level up the food chain? Why don't you? Discover how you can raise the level of your presentations. You can be more professional in how your package your proposals. Deliver your ideas in such a way that your contacts would feel comfortable showing your proposal to the CEO of their company. Out-think and out-work your competition and you'll see some progress.

2 WAYS TO FIND YOUR WHY

1. FIND IT INSIDE

Trust Your Gut
Know your values
Allow moments of 'awe'
Listen. To yourself.
Be for the sake of being.
Love for the sake of loving.

2. WORK AT FINDING IT

Bring an open mind.
Write it down.
Keep working at it.
Dig deep.
Make yourself cry.
Get to know yourself.

My Why: *"To challenge and inspire people so that we can discover our full potential"*

CHAPTER 9

TWO WAYS TO FIND YOUR WHY?

DO YOU KNOW your "why?" Why are you doing what you are doing? Please don't tell me to make money. Money is a result of what you are doing, it is not the why. Your "why" is your purpose. When you find your purpose and live it, you discover meaning and you get to do what you love. When you do what you love, you never have to work a day in your life.

When you find your passion and your purpose and live out your "why", your work becomes a labor of love. Work is what we do by the hour, while Labor sets its own pace. Living out your mission, you tap into a creative stream that allows you flow—an intense focus and crisp sense of clarity that others notice. Simon Sinek has a TED Talk video (find it on You Tube—How Great Leaders Inspire Action) with more than 53 million views on YouTube in which he explains the importance of finding your "why". He points out that "people don't buy what you do; they buy why you do it. And what you do simply proves what you believe."

What is your cause? What are your beliefs that drive you and get you out of bed every morning? Why should anyone care? Most of us can explain what we do. Most of us can explain how we do what we do. But can you articulate your "why"? Are you passionate about solving problems? Are you driven by continuous improvement? Does helping others succeed drive you? Are you trying to make the industry more professional? Do you love being part of the creative process and watching an idea germinate, blossom and flourish? Find YOUR Why and live it courageously. Steve Jobs said, "the only way to be truly satisfied is to do what you believe is great work. And the only way to do great work is to love what you do. Don't settle."

It is your responsibility to discover your "why". Once discovered, center your life on it and allow it to flood meaning into your life goals and daily activities and become an everyday source of integrity and pride. Your purpose should be rooted in love, not fear; aligned with your fundamentals, your passions and desires; something that moves you emotionally and not just mentally; be energizing and nourishing; inspiring and worth building a life around.

Here are two ways to help you find your "why".

1. You'll find it inside. You already know the answer, but you will find it close. So, step back and look inward and then trust your gut. Let go of self-interest and control and reflect with honesty on your values, your beliefs and the things that matter most to you. Ask yourself if your life serves something of value in itself and not just what you think you can get from it. If you can direct your energies in the service of creating a greater good, it will return to you. Allow yourself to have moments of "awe" that put you into the moment. Watch the leaves change color and drift to the ground. Stare at the fire and smell the smoke and hear the pops and crackles. (Hopefully around a campfire or fire pit). Get up and watch the sunrise and see how the colors of the world change and hear the birds greet the new day. And then, listen. To yourself. The answer is inside of you.

   BE FOR THE SAKE OF BEING. LOVE FOR THE SAKE OF LOVING. GIVE FOR THE SAKE OF GIVING. Trust the world to give it back to you. It always does. It's the law. The law of the universe. Pursue your purpose with a sense of service to it. When you keep your self-interest at bay, you're able to find your true purpose.

2. You'll find it by working at finding it. Steve Pavlina suggests that anyone can do it in about twenty minutes. Begin with an open mind and a commitment to work at it until you get there. On a blank piece of paper or a new document file if you're more of a computer person, write "what is my true purpose in life?" Write the first answer that pops into your head. Now repeat that with each new answer that you think of. When you get to the one that makes you cry, you have found it.

It could take you one hundred, two hundred or even a thousand answers but when you hit one that hits every emotional nerve in your body, you will have found it.

Will finding your "why" help your business? It will if you make the decision to live it, love it and be it.

Be for the sake of being.
Love for the sake of loving.
Give for the sake of giving.

THIS ONE THING.

1

You have unlimited

POWER

to allow yourself to create

BEAUTY, LOVE AND ART

in the way that you live.

You can be that

CREATIVE FORCE

by doing one thing

BE YOU NOW!

CHAPTER 10
THIS ONE THING. CREATE.

MAKE THIS WORLD a better place. Make this industry a better place. Make your home a better place. You can do it. Starting with you.

A few years ago, I lived in downtown Chicago and joined Michigan Avenue Toastmasters. This was a diverse group of interesting people all dedicated to becoming better speakers and helping each other elevate their skills. I took the #3 Bus up to the Magnificent Mile and cut through Water Tower Place to the Hotel Seneca every Tuesday evening. It was exciting, inspiring and motivating. When I moved to Grand Rapids, I joined a Tuesday night Toastmasters Club that met at the same time but in a retirement home and with a handful of people and very little of the energy or excitement to which I was accustomed. When I whined about this to one of my Chicago friends, he replied, "Well, it sounds like you've got your work cut out for you."

What incredible advice! It echoed the sentiment of Mahatma Gandhi who said, "You must be the change that you want to see in the world." We spend so much time fretting, worrying, complaining about things we don't like. Instead, do the one or two small things that you can that will make a difference.

We have unlimited power to allow ourselves to create beauty, love and art in the way that we live. You can be that creative force by doing one thing—BE YOU NOW.

Your gift is to be yourself—fully, fantastically and consciously—in this moment. Of course, you must love yourself to share yourself.

You have everything that you need in this moment. So why should you worry? Worry is a fantasyland that you've made up and are suffering in even though it does not exist. If you believe that you know the future, life has not yet taught you just how quickly your life can change. You can believe in now. Indeed, it is the reality that there is, and it is perfect.

The past is just as fabled. It is gone. It's yesterday's wind. Living with regrets, or worse, living with grudges, resentments or hatred over past events diminishes you and causes suffering. Let go of the negativity from past events and discover the grace of forgiveness. It is something you do for yourself, not for the object of your negativity

We get to choose our thoughts. We get to choose our attitudes. Choose wisely.

Learn to love and to live with the awesome power that love gives you. Fear is the opposite of love and fear is learned. Marianne Williamson said, "Love is what we are born with. Fear is what we learn. Love is the essential reality and our purpose on earth. To be consciously aware of it, to experience love in ourselves and others, is the meaning of life. Meaning does not lie in things. Meaning lies in us."

If you don't love what you do, why are you doing it? You only get to go around once in this life, so make sure you're doing it right. There is no dress rehearsal. This is it. You can create a better world, a better industry, a better company, a better family, a better you. Choose to create beautiful moments through your every interaction, your every choice.

SUMMIT
REACHING THE PEAK OF YOUR POTENTIAL

Part 2: 10 Strategies to Thrive in Any Economy

CHAPTER 11:
POSITIVITY · ASK · INSPIRE · NEGOTIATE
(THE FIRST FOUR STEPS OF PAIN RELIEF)

CHAPTER 12: REINVENT
(THE NEXT STEP TO PAIN RELIEF)

CHAPTER 13: EVALUATE · LIVE · INNOVATE
(3 MORE STEPS TO PAIN RELIEF)

CHAPTER 14: ENDURE · FUTURE
(FINAL TWO STEPS TO PAIN RELIEF)

CHAPTER 15: SEIZE THE OPPORTUNITY

CHAPTER 16: ARE YOU READY FOR THE GOOD THINGS TO HAPPEN?

CHAPTER 17: WHAT NEW SKILLS WILL YOU NEED TO SUCCEED IN THE NEW ECONOMY?

CHAPTER 18: LESSONS FROM "THE GREAT ONE"

CHAPTER 19: SCARY STUFF - INNOVATE OR DIE

CHAPTER 20: WHEN WILL YOU START?

PAIN RELIEF
10 STRATEGIES TO THRIVE IN ANY ECONOMY

P — POSITIVITY
A — ASK
I — INSPIRE
N — NEGOTIATE

R — REINVENT
E — EVALUATE
L — LIVE
I — INNOVATE
E — ENDURE
F — FUTURE

CHAPTER 11
POSITIVITY • ASK • INSPIRE • NEGOTIATE (THE FIRST FOUR STEPS TO PAIN RELIEF)

CREATING PROSPERITY IS a result of creating value. Your attitude is one of the easiest ways that you can do your part to create a healthier economy. Incentive professional, Jim Dittman said, "Recessions start and end with attitude. They occur when enough people believe they will occur. They end when enough people believe they will end." I believe that.

Positivity is the first and most important strategy for fighting back and allowing abundance to flow again. You can make positivity your personal habit by closely monitoring your words and actions. Don't allow yourself to go negative. Keep Chicken Little out of your world! Control your culture by not allowing negativity and by modeling positivity. Find genuine positives and reasons to praise. Reconnect with your abundance which is inside of you. By counting your blessings and living your gratitude, the less you lack. Remember, you become your thoughts. You have a choice— scarcity thinking or abundance believing.

Your next home runs—your biggest successes—are in your customer's needs not yet met. If you can't find them, you're not looking very hard. The second strategy is **ASK**. Ask your customers what their biggest needs are. Ask them one-on-one. Ask them through surveys, focus groups, special events, contests or any interactive thing you can think of. But ASK them. Let them know that you care that you want to help, that you are part of their team. Perform a value-added "audit" of your past work so you can review with them what they've bought in the past and how you can better serve them in the future. Learn how to think like them. Watch how they go to market. Ask your employees and partners to help you learn about your customers. Ask for referrals and go deeper within an organization. Develop champions who can help you to find their pain points and the people that you need to know to better serve them. Consider creating a Mastermind group that you can ask, bounce ideas off of and get fresh outsider insight.

Especially in today's business environment, people are looking for inspiration. You can **INSPIRE** your customers, your community, your employees and in so doing, yourself. The word means "In Spirit." There is a divine quality to exercising your inspiration muscles. During an earlier recession (1975), Coca-Cola came out with an upbeat, inspiration advertising campaign, "Have Coke and a Smile." And they grew their business. Now is the time to become more charitable. Give your way out of the funk. If you can't give money, give time, give ideas, give hope. You have a prosperity garden. Cultivate it and cultivate abundance.

Inspire through your example. Now is the time to increase YOUR marketing activity. Now is when you should be demonstrating the power of your medium. Inspire through sponsorships of great causes. You have all of the tools and in addition to doing good, you'll meet other likeminded, success-oriented, abundance believing prospects.

Our 35th president, John F. Kennedy said, "Let us never **NEGOTIATE** out of fear. But let us never fear to negotiate." I believe in abundance and I believe that negotiation is all about creating win-win scenarios. Becoming a true and a good partner with your clients, with your employees and with your suppliers puts all of the wheels of success into motion. You are all interdependent and the more trust and true value that you can focus on delivering to each of the cogs in your success wheel, the further you will go.

On the more practical and tactical side of this coin, now is the time to negotiate with your lenders. Lock in long-term interest rates, make sure your credit lines are established and secure. Your landlord may be willing to renegotiate your lease to keep your business. Keep a close eye on your receivables. Have a plan to make sure your customers are paying you according to your terms. My process was to call my clients ten days after an invoice was sent under the guise of a service follow-up call. I would ask if they were completely satisfied and make sure there were no issues with the promotion. Then would come the after-thought Colombo-style question, "Oh, by the way. Did you get our invoice? Do you have any questions about it? Is it in the system and scheduled for payment?" This simple process reduced our days-to-pay from over 40+ to 32. Remember, it isn't a sale until their check clears. And the sales experience isn't over until the customer has received an accurate and timely invoice and been happy to pay you for it.

Negotiate new partnerships. For your customers, think about who their target audience is and about non-competitors of theirs that you might be able to create a joint promotion for. Your client gets shared costs, and you get a new customer in the deal. Similarly, think about your own company. Who is out there trying to reach the same customers as you are? Who has similar values and culture that you might be able to partner with? Is there a trade show company, an event planner, ad agencies or even other advertising media that you may be able to create a new partnership with? A few years ago, I partnered with a radio station and a restaurant creating a "best bosses" event. The premise was that employees would phone or write in why their boss deserved a TGIF Party in his honor at the restaurant. The restaurant would host the event, give the company participants a promotional product and free appetizers. The radio station also gave out promotional products at the party. We got two promotional product clients and exposure to the local business community. The radio station got a restaurant client, interaction within the business community and listenership at businesses. And the restaurant brought in groups of 10—20 customers early after work who would not normally be there and many who would stay for additional food or even dinner.

Win-win-win.

Receiving PPAI Hall of Fame Induction just 25 days after removal of a malignant colorectal tumor.

CHAPTER 12
REINVENT (THE NEXT STEP TO PAIN RELIEF)

WHAT IS YOUR value proposition in this new reality? Have your customers' needs changed? You need to reinvent yourself to be relevant to the needs of your marketplace. For many reinvention simply means gaining clarity of purpose and a resolve to live out that purpose.

Why do your customers need you? Until you get very clear on this—and the emphasis here is YOU—you are at risk. Because if there is no need, there are no customers. If you have no customers, you have no sales. If you have no sales, you have no business. Period. It is that simple. Constantly define the need and why you are the person to solve it.

What can you be best in the world at? What are your strengths? Yes, this sounds like Business Plan 101, but go there with me and take it to the next level. Pick one thing that you are best at—where you can show a demonstrable difference—and start building on it. It may be subtle, but it is important. For Apple, it has been and continues to be design. For Walgreens it is convenient locations. For Starbucks it is 85,000 different ways to customize your coffee experience. Fick one attribute that you can claim and make it holy.

What are you not so good at? Just because you can do something, doesn't mean you should. Stick to your core competencies and find trusted partners to do the rest. The strength of the promotional products' system of distribution channels—manufacturers to suppliers to distributors to end buyers—is uniquely set up for each to specialize in what they can do best. When you start dabbling into areas that are outside of your core strengths, you are diluting your value proposition. Deliver your best work and hire experts to do theirs and you will deliver more value to your customers.

"A clear plan relieves you of the torment of choice" Saul Bellow

Get very clear about who you are, what you do and how you do it. Develop a simple marketing plan that will make decision making easy. Who you are? Who you sell to? What problems do you solve? How do you go to market? Know the answers to these critical questions and resist any temptation to deviate in the least.

Knowing your value proposition requires a knowledge of who your customers are and what they need. You can articulate what you deliver to these customers and how you do it. You can tell anyone how you are different from your competition. You can state what a customer can expect by choosing you. Reinvent your company to be the pain relief they need.

"Many options are not transparent.
They need to be explored and evaluated with care.
What you see is not always what you get."
— J. Grant Howard, Balancing Life's Demands: A New Perspective on Priorities

"You must live in the present, launch yourself on every wave, find your eternity in each moment. Fools stand on their island opportunities and look toward another land. There is no other land, there is no other life but this."
~ Henry David Thoreau

"If you have always done it that way,
it is probably wrong.
Charles Kettering

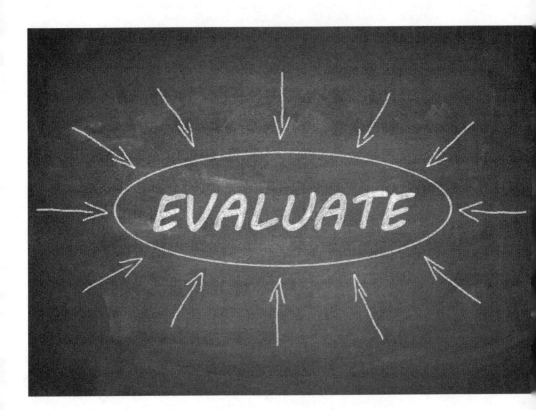

CHAPTER 13
EVALUATE · LIVE · INNOVATE (THREE MORE STEPS TO PAIN RELIEF)

NORMAL IS DEAD. Deal with it. You need to be evaluating everything in your business. EVALUATE: What's your purpose? What are today's numbers? Why aren't customers buying? What are prospects buying? Where are the big wins? We all know that sales are a numbers game. If the numbers have changed, what does that mean to your business. Remember, you're dealing with today, not yesterday.

Revisit your prospecting processes. Who do you want to work for? What types of customers will appreciate your unique approach to solving their problems? Have a Target List and work it with specific actions daily, weekly, monthly, quarterly and annually. What markets appear strong and growing? Education, health care, franchises, auto repair shops, rental properties, green industries, casinos and lottery, entertainment, consignment and thrift stores, credit unions and community banks and biotech are all segments that seem to be doing well right now. Have you called on any of these types of companies?

When you EVALUATE you learn how to create value by focusing with clarity about your purpose, your business, your vision and the road to fulfill your vision.

LIVE right now. In the midst of all of this change, turmoil, negativity and ambiguity. This is strategy number seven of ten on dealing with the change all around you. So, take a minute and breathe. Don't try to do everything all at once. Take care of yourself. You need to be strong, healthy, positive and growing.

You do have a lot to do. But don't just spend your time. Invest it. Stop the obligation attitude of "I got to do this" and "I should do that" and start looking at just how blessed you are to be able to do those things. Interrupting your important business activities to pick up a child from school or a practice is a blessing. Count it. There are lots of people who would love to be able to do those "got-to's" that you complain about. Your richest moments are your relationship moments. Never let go of that.

Learning to live in the moment, or more correctly—relearning how to live in the moment—is something that will make a huge difference for every aspect of your life. But especially for your inner peace and ending the suffering and drama you create. Take your cue from little kids. They know how to be real and be now. Forget who you were and focus on who you can be. Follow the changeless—your values, ideals, dreams and operating principles. Deepen the power and possibility of all of your relationships and work on becoming self-directed, self-managed and self-motivated. Live a three-legged life with a balance of your home, work and self relationships and responsibilities.

The eighth strategy is Innovate. Innovate means find new ways of doing something. That's where the big wins are going to be. Be on a constant search for new ways to relieve the pain points of your customers and you'll be well on your way to market leadership and success. With all of the talk of the slump in retailing, have you visited your local Apple store lately? They're packed. The stores are packed with people excited about innovation. When did Apple open their first retail store? During the recession of 2001. Who would have believed that one day we would be able to carry our entire library of music in our pocket? That we would buy music not in music stores but over the internet? And when did Apple introduce the iPod? During the recession of 2001. Know where you want your company to be when the recovery begins and go there now!

We innovate best when we forget about sales and focus on creating value. Find new ways to create for your clients: solutions that help them eliminate their dangers, capture their opportunities and reinforce their strengths. Robert Schuler posed the ageless question: What would you do if you knew you could not fail? Timidity is not a road to success. Remember what the great Gretzky said, "you miss 100% of the shots you don't take." Look for products, services and ideas that scale. What can you be doing that does not increase your need for people and costs in direct proportion to your revenue? How can you be working smarter and getting more for the efforts you perform every day anyway?

To innovate means that you need to learn to get comfortable with discomfort. When you're talking about new, you're talking about change.

Rename anxiety opportunity. Train yourself that when you feel anxiety to welcome it as a sign that a new opportunity is presenting itself. These are troubling times, but you can turn trouble into transformation!

Innovate because there has never been a better time. Innovate because the market needs pain relief! Create to be great!

CHAPTER 14
ENDURE • FUTURE (THE FINAL TWO STEPS TO PAIN RELIEF

Success is a marathon, not a sprint. Endurance is critical in any endeavor in which you wish to be one of the best. That means you better love what you're doing because I don't think that endurance is possible without passion. In his great new book, Outliers, Malcolm Gladwell provides several examples of the 10,000-hour rule. The Beatles, for example, were so good because of the eight-hour gigs that they played night after night in Germany before their "instant" success. So, the ninth strategy is ENDURE.

You need to commit to be the best. Why live small? To be the best you need to focus on being the best. And this means taking daily steps toward large goals, having planned weekly activities that move you from good to great. The difference is not big. Just do one more thing. Make one more phone call. Send out one hand-written thank you note. Make a point to recognize one kind act or stellar performance. You don't need to be a lot better than your competition—just a little bit. The difference of one stroke in a major golf tournament can mean a half million dollars to the player. The difference between fourth place and gold in many Olympic events is measured in hundredths of a second.

Enduring does mean having a process and following it. For me this meant a process for prospecting and a process for getting that first call. An introductory mailing was followed by a first phone call, followed by a more detailed mailing and a friendly follow-up phone call. These steps were followed up with a creative mailing demonstrating my own craft and the third phone call after that usually resulted in the appointment and start of a new relationship. Endurance requires passion and it requires commitment. Nobody said it was easy. Most worthwhile things aren't. But one thing is sure—somebody is making the impossible reality because they are committed and are doing it.

I always hated to run. But I was committed to not being grossly overweight. I've always been a large-framed person and when I quit smoking cigarettes, saw the effects of heart disease on my father and decided I didn't want to have my chest split open—I decided to run. My journal shows an entry that I "tried to run 100 yards." The next day's entry says, "jogged 150 yards." The start of my journey to running twenty 26.2-mile marathons including Boston, New York, Chicago and others in twelve states began by trying to run from one telephone pole to the next. That goal became the goal to run a mile. That goal became the goal to run a 5k (3.1 miles) and then a 10k and then a 25k and finally the full marathon. There were always reasons to quit but I chose to endure. I never measured myself against those who ran along with me. I measured myself against those who never had the courage to start.

And finally, my tenth and final strategy to Thrive in Any Economy is to never fear the Future. Just be sure that you are creating it. Hire youth and learn from them. The old days of hiring young people and teaching them are past. It's not a one-way street. They can teach you how to be meeting the needs of your customers of today and tomorrow. Jim Collins, author of Good to Great says of this new generation, "They have a sense of responsibility and service and a lack of cynicism that is remarkable and wonderful." And I agree. My presentations using Keynote, were made possible by coaching from four brilliant Apple store employees who taught me so much about how to reach an audience and who learned a few good business and relationship tips from me.

Your business needs to be focused on the WHO. Who are you working with? Who are your employees, clients and partners? Again, Jim Collins says, "If you cannot predict the *what*, you have to be able to do a good job with the *who*, because the *what* is going to be constantly shifting." You need to create a culture of people who share a set of values, have very clear responsibilities and who love to perform.

The world is changing. Adapt and adopt. In this web 2.0 world, your customers become a part of your company. What are you doing about that? In a world where corporate social responsibility and the environment are playing a bigger and bigger role in missions and directions, how are you addressing this? When a simple industry like promotional products is now being limited and regulated in the healthcare and pharmaceutical areas, have you thought about how to solve the problems that this is causing for your clients? It's not so simple anymore—CPSIA, General Conformity Certificates, Product Safety, Age Gradings, Lead, Recalls, C-TPAT, Prop 65, traceability, third party testing—these are all now part of your world. Can you embrace change rather than simply endure it?

Focus on today and the future will take care of itself. Because neither the past nor the future even exist. You create the future through today's contributions, plans, achievements and commitments. Focus on these twenty-four hours and you will become the best futurist ever!

So, there you have it. Ten Strategies to Strive in Any Economy.

Positivity

Ask

Inspire

Negotiate

Reinvent

Evalute

Live

Innovate

Endure

Future

PAIN RELIEF. Remember, there has never in our lifetimes been a moment of more opportunity than there is right now. Problem solvers always make money. Find the Pain. Be the Aspirin.

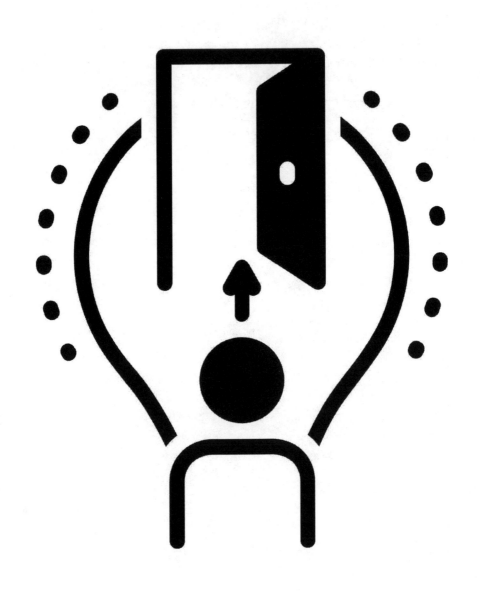

CHAPTER 15
SEIZE THE OPPORTUNITY

IF YOU ARE going to thrive in any economy, you must commit yourself to a laser-like focus on doing first things first and a ferocious understanding of what you are NOT going to do. For me, having a Stop Doing List has become more important than my To Do List. Here's what works for me. After twenty-three years of starting, building, growing, merging and leading a successful distributorship and promotion agency, I was at a point in my life where I wanted to reinvent myself.

My Do and STOP Do List has four parts. I identified twelve things that I love doing. The list includes reading, collaborating, leading, speaking and traveling. I specified seven things that I hate doing which became my STOP DOING list. This has been invaluable to me when opportunities have presented themselves that may have had potential financial rewards but had the potential to drain my happiness and personal peace. I also listed ten things that I'm good at, that I have proven accomplishments and successes that I feel great about. Some of these duplicate the items on my "Love Doing" list and some are more specific disciplines. I know that I'm very good at incentive marketing, at promotional marketing, at writing, speaking and facilitation and these are on this list. Here again, I can compare opportunities against this list and see if it will allow me to perform at a high level and from my strengths. The fourth part of my list details concepts and core values that I am passionate about. Things like professionalism, creativity, innovation, integrity and transparency.

By becoming clear with yourself about who you are, what you stand for, what you want to do and importantly, what you don't want to do, you can develop a laser focus on your strengths and on the things that you can be successful at. You've given yourself a standard against which you can measure opportunities and challenges and areas where you need to improve.

At all times, you must baby your customers. Now is when you need to make sure that your best customers know just how much you love them.

And like a baby, nurture them. Give them value-adds. Give them values and specials that make them feel valued and special. I'm not a big proponent of discounting but rewarding an existing customer with a gift certificate for their next purchase is a powerful strategy in a market where your competition may be offering cut-throat pricing in order to get in the door. Remember that you have the relationship, and you can protect it by how you make your customers FEEL. Make them feel special, valued and smart for working with you.

There are two significant areas where you can focus to increase your value. How can you differentiate your competitive position? And how can you make yourself more relevant to the needs of your customers? What reports can you provide your customers that your competition cannot? How can you learn more about solving your customers problems? How can you be a more irreplaceable member of your clients' teams? You have a personality, a level of creativity, a compassion and passion that no one else can match.

In the promotional products business, being able to find a product or get it delivered quickly is not much of a competitive differentiator. How can you differentiate yourself? Often, the ways that you can find to make yourself more relevant to the needs of your clients are the things that will also differentiate you from your competition.

Carpe Diem and also Seize the New Opportunities. Traditional media is losing market share to interactive promotional media. Promotional products may be an old media, but we've never been traditional. And we've never been more relevant to reach target audiences. These challenges mean great opportunity. You may be able to partner with media that you once thought of as competition. A promotional product offered in a newspaper ad, outdoor campaign, radio station event can help them prove the capabilities of their media. But you'll be doing it through the power of ours. On the other side of this decline of traditional media, you can look for media that you can pick up budget from. Those are prospects for a medium that "remains to be seen" when their customers are looking for their services. Find riches in niches. Think differently and you'll find new opportunities. Seize them.

CHAPTER 16
ARE YOU READY FOR GOOD THINGS TO HAPPEN?

THERE IS SO much negativity that it is easy to miss the opportunity. These are times that should be making you very, very excited. There has never been a moment in history since you've been on this earth where there has been greater opportunity for great success. You just need to go out and create it!

You can "create to be great" by recognizing the immense amount of pain in the marketplace and then going out there and being the pain relief. Focus on becoming a problem solver. Problem solvers ALWAYS make money. What is it your clients and prospects need right now? Think in terms of what they need and then get creative. You have experts all around you who want to help create solutions. Your supplier partners, your industry colleagues, your association friends—all of them want to help you help your clients.

Re-think your elevator speech. People have told you to have a thirty-second pitch. How about seven seconds? What problem do you solve? No one wants to hear about your products. They want to know—what problem can you solve for them. Can you help them increase sales? Lower costs? Reactivate old accounts? Start a loyalty program? Recruit the best talent? Build a better brand?

Now is the time to be targeting new prospects. Why? Because they are looking for problem solvers. Your competition may be biting their nails and buying into all the negativity. It is a great time for you to be the new thinking, the innovator, the creator of solutions that prospects are looking for desperately right now! If you don't have any problems to solve, you're just not in the game.

Become the master of the positive. You don't need to be a carrier of the negativity disease. Become the deliverer of good news. It's a matter of believing in abundance instead of scarcity. There is still just as much abundance in this world today as there was last year and the year before that—more actually. Grab a hold of it and be determined to be an abundance thinker and a positivity carrier. You can make a difference by being the difference.

It's really easy to focus on the wrong things in difficult economic times. But if you begin to focus on ANYTHING BUT YOUR CUSTOMER'S NEEDS, you cannot create value. You cannot hate a competitor enough to improve your performance. You cannot deliver value when you're focused on fear, scarcity, loss and negativity. The need for you is out there if you are out there to solve problems and be the pain relief.

"When you need to innovate, you need collaboration."
MARISSA MEYER

"Without leaps of imagination or dreaming, we lose the excitement of possibilities. Dreaming, after all is a form of planning."
GLORIA STEINEM

"The problem with the race to the bottom is that you might win."
SETH GODIN

"Authenticity is a collection of choices that we have to make every day. It's about the choice to show up and be real. The choice to be honest. The choice to let out true selves be seen."
BRENE BROWN

"Resilience is accepting your new reality, even if it's less good than the one you had before. You can fight it, you can do nothing but scream about what you've lost, or you can accept that and try to put together something that's good."
ELIZABETH EDWARDS

CHAPTER 17
WHAT NEW SKILLS WILL YOU NEED TO SUCCEED IN THE NEW ECONOMY?

This changes everything. That is one way of looking at the perfect storm of an international pandemic, a faltering economy, the technological revolution, full-scale globalization, values shift, and generational changes that have come together all at once. Not only have the rules changed, but the game is changed. Here are six new skills that are required of you to play in this New Economy.

Shift from product sales to idea sales to program sales to process sales. What does that mean? It means that if you've been making your living by showing and selling product, you're going to want to learn a few new steps to dance to. Product sales focuses on the stuff. It is all about the client having a pre-existing need and delivering a product to fill the need. Moving to idea sales, you identify a client need—perhaps one they weren't even aware of—and deliver a product-based solution including a way to distribute and measure. You've just moved from need fulfillment to need creation. When you move to program selling, you are holding product and ideas accountable to a goal, using promotional techniques such as consumer promotions, incentive programs, safety programs or employee retention and recognition. When you move up to process selling, you are getting deep into the needs and methods of operation of your client. You are tailoring your solutions to work with their operations to save them money, to make their operation run more smoothly and to become an indispensable member of their team.

1. Learn to think in terms of Collaboration rather than Competition. When you are thinking in terms of what best solves your client's needs, you may realize that you can help them the most by sticking with what you do best. Find and

collaborate with their other agencies, including your competition, to create the most powerful pool of talent and expertise. Learn to respect and trust and you may be surprised how it comes right back to you in equal measure.

2. Move from seat of the pants to planning with flexibility. Just because the rate of change may seem like chaos, does not mean that you don't need to plan. Planning is still critical. But execution must be flexible. Situations change quickly and being able to recognize when to zig and when to zag will be a competitive advantage.

3. Let's stop the Race to the Bottom and Race to the Top! Why do so many of us toe the line and take off running when the race is to the bottom? Do you really want to be known as the cheapest? One of the biggest reasons to get out of the product selling game is that commoditization is a zero-sum game with no winners. The low-price buyer loses the opportunity to work with the best. They risk their brand's reputation. They miss deadlines. They become acquainted with disappointment. Set your vision and your sights on becoming the best in the business. Race to become a problem solver, a results-getter, a revenue enhancer and a brand builder.

4. Why would you want to be a poor imitation of someone else? What can you be best in the world at? Find it and be it. You'll be the one, the only, the original you! Your personality, your experience, your creativity, your problem-solving skills—these are your competitive advantages. We all have access to the same stuff, from the same suppliers, with the same lead times, for the same price. Differentiation is THE things that will set you apart and create wild demand for your services. You are the only thing that only YOU can deliver. Create your brand and create demand for it.

5. Resilience is a necessary skill in this economy. With change advancing at accelerating paces and with no end in sight, you

are bound to be knocked down. Getting knocked down is to be expected. You only lose when you stop getting back up. People love the old cliche' about making lemonade when life hands you lemons. But I have news for you. You'll need more than lemons to make lemonade. You'll need some rock-solid core values that remain steady no matter how rocky life becomes. You'll need a clear vision of where you are going. If you know where you're going, you'll be able to get back up when down and get right back on the right path to lead you there. Understand that life doesn't play fair and that success may not come easy. Learn to accept what life brings and keep moving forward to your goals and where you want to end up.

Success in the new economy requires continuous improvement. It requires a commitment to excellence. It means you need to be always learning. You must be passionate about creating value.

CHAPTER 18
LESSONS FROM "THE GREAT ONE"

It's up to you to create your future. Tough times require tough performances. Tough times bring out champions. The greatest hockey player in the history of the game—the Great One—Wayne Gretzky was deemed, "too small, too wiry, and too slow to be a force in the NHL" by the so-called experts. But he has a lot to teach us about creating greatness. Here are some quotes by the Great One that we can learn from...

"The highest compliment that you can pay me is to say that I work hard every day, that I never dog it." Gretzky was playing against ten-year old's when he was only six years old. He learned to be tough and always perform at his highest level. When you're working at creating value for your clients, you must constantly be delivering your very best game. When you're working, work hard. Have a plan and apply your skills and your very unique creativity and personality to the best of your ability and you'll "never dog it."

Gretzky was also a bit obsessive over his hockey sticks. He didn't like his touching any others or crossing. He even put baby powder on the ends. "I think it's essentially a matter of taking care of what takes care of you." When it comes to your profession, your livelihood, are you "taking care of what takes care of you?" Your best clients, your best suppliers, your best employees—how are you taking care of them? Your best clients deserve your best work. Your best suppliers deserve your highest loyalty and an on-going spirit of cooperation and partnership. Your best employees deserve your appreciation, recognition and your personal mentoring and development. And how about your industry? You can take care of your industry by giving back through your regional and international association. A strong industry requires your participation, your voice, your votes and your volunteerism.

"You miss 100% of the shots you don't take." A weak economy is no reason to not be taking your best shot every day. You can't make sales if you don't make calls. You can't open new accounts without risking some rejection. Your closing percentages may be way down. Take more shots!

"Procrastination is one of the most common and deadliest of diseases and its toll on success and happiness is heavy." If you're waiting for a better economy, waiting for a nicer day, waiting for something in the future—you are creating nothing. To create value, you must do it in the only reality there is—right this moment. When you are working—WORK! Turn off your email for an hour. Let Facebook rest for the morning—your friends will be there later. Setting goals is important but taking action steps right now will move you closer to making a score and winning.

Of all of the Gretzky quotes, my personal favorite is: "I skate to where the puck is going to be, not where it has been." Many of us are still playing by the rules of the game of business as they were in 2018 or 2019 (or 1975 for some!). The puck has moved and it's not coming back. The reality is that the Recovery (when it comes) will not bring you back. You must be moving out to meet it. You must also create value for your customers by helping them see where the puck is going to be and meeting it. You do that by constantly improving your skills, by looking for new ways to create relevant solutions and innovative new strategies. Where do you want to be when the recovery comes? Skate over there now.

CHAPTER 19
SCARY STUFF – INNOVATE OR DIE

What are you going to do now that is going to make you even more relevant in five years? What are you going to do to create the customer experience needed to assure that you can compete and flourish long term?

Are you going to curse the online challengers who are driving you crazy? Or are you going to outthink them, out serve them and make yourself irreplaceable to your clients?

How are you going to write the story that your customers will want to be a part of?

You don't need to fade away. You just need to deliver on the new expectations of your customers who are being spoiled by disrupters like Amazon. This is no time to be resting on your past accomplishments. Kodak did and a company with who on March 31, 1999 employed 83,000 people and had market capitalization of almost $21 Billion Dollars went bankrupt while a little company with 12 employees and no revenues was purchased by Facebook for $1 Billion Dollars in 2012 (Instagram). Kodak failed to innovate and stubbornly stuck to film as the world turned digital. (Can you guess who invented digital photography? Yes, it was Kodak.)

Your customers are getting younger and you probably are not. But that doesn't mean your thinking needs to stay stuck in the past. Learn new skills. Accept the fact that your customers are going to research online. They're going to look for reviews online. They may prefer that you communicate with them through text messages rather than phone or email.

You must avoid the fates of AOL, Blockbuster, Barnes and Noble and MySpace. Focus on what your customers want and concentrate on reinventing yourself constantly. That is work that is never done. You can be the disrupter. You can be the leader. Write your new story. The story about how you do the hard work of innovating daily to create more value and more meaning for your customers.

It's your choice. Innovate or else.

"You don't need to be great to start, but you have to start to be great"
ZIG ZIGLAR

"If you love life, don't waste time, for time is what life is made up of"
BRUCE LEE

"One hour per day of study in your chosen field is all it takes. One hour per day of study will put you at the top of your field within three years. Within five years you'll be a national authority. In seven years, you can be one of the best people in the world at what you do."
EARL NIGHTINGALE

CHAPTER 20
WHEN WILL YOU START?

TIME. IT'S HERE and it's gone. There are lots of cliche's about time and there ain't no time like the present. So, let's get going. And let's get growing. Ask yourself "When" at least three times.

When will I create the business of my dreams? If you can't describe your business that way, then why are you still doing the same things over and over again and expecting a different result? What would need to change to get you to change? The only way to get the results that you want is to be taking positive steps toward your dreams now. You will need to focus. You will need to schedule. When will you prospect? When will you research your prospects? When will you plan? When will you identify the critical things you need to do to build your business and then actually schedule them? You need to make appointments for yourself to tackle the important action items needed to make your vision a reality.

When will I stop wasting time? Your time is your inventory. Your time is your most precious asset. In *The 7 Habits of Highly Effective People*, Stephen Covey described four quadrants: Important and Urgent—These are the critical activities that will drive results, create happy clients, solve problems and move your sales needle. You want to be in this space as much as possible. Important and Not Urgent is the second quadrant. This is where you are prospecting, creating presentations, planning, building important relationships and laying the groundwork for the results you're seeking. You need to schedule these items. If the activity doesn't fall into one of those two categories, delegate it or drop it. Quadrant 3 is Interruptions—things that may be urgent, but not important. If you can delegate any of these things, you'll be way ahead of the game. Interruptions can be phone calls, some mail, some email, some social media and even some fun or popular activities. Distractions fall into Quadrant 4. Just don't go there when you've got a business to build. Distractions can include busywork, trivial matters, time wasters, rabbit holes and for many of us the internet.

When will I learn new skills? We live in a time of great change. We need to not just accept change; we need to embrace it. I consider skill development a Quadrant 2 activity that needs to be scheduled. It is Important but not as urgent as closing a sale. This is where you plant the seeds that you will harvest later. Our focus needs to be on what our customers need and will be needing. It's the customer's perspective that matters and the Platinum Rule applies. We need to give them what they want, not what we would want. Your customers want to be reached in new ways today. This means you may need to learn how to use social media (gasp!). You may need to become more proficient at communicating through text messages. What worked yesterday will probably not work today. You need to be on a course of continuous improvement. Continuing education needs to be a part of your life if you want to be relevant tomorrow.

Your time is your most valuable asset. Use it wisely. When? Now!

SUMMIT
REACHING THE PEAK OF YOUR POTENTIAL

Part 3: 10 Success Strategies You Need Now

CHAPTER 21:
SUCCESS HABITS IN THE AGE OF COVID-19

CHAPTER 22: THEY'RE STILL BUYING (IMPART)

CHAPTER 23: THINGS ARE CHANGING. WHETHER FOR THE GOOD OR THE BAD IS UP TO YOU.

CHAPTER 24: FIVE MINDSET ADJUSTMENTS YOU NEED TO MAKE NOW.

CHAPTER 25: COVID-19: THIS TOO IS A DEFINING MOMENT

CHAPTER 26: FIND YOUR FOCUS

CHAPTER 27: QUIT TRYING TO BE EVERYTHING TO EVERYONE

CHAPTER 28: ARE YOU BETTER THAN YOU WERE YESTERDAY?

CHAPTER 29: IF YOU DON'T KNOW, HOW WILL THEY KNOW?

CHAPTER 30: TO INCREASE YOUR SALES — QUIT SELLING!

CHAPTER 21
THE SUCCESS HABITS IN THE AGE OF COVID-19

Way back in 1989, Steven Covey wrote one of the top-selling business and self-help books ever published, "*The 7 Habits of Highly Effective People.*" These seven principals are worth revisiting today during this time of fear, change, unpredictability and uncertainty. If you've never read it, or if like me it's been a decade, here they are with some Kiewiet Commentary.

Be Proactive. Respond to current events positively with a mind to improve your situation. Don't sit and wait to react. Take action now to move in the direction of your goals and objectives.

Begin with the end in mind. This is extremely important today. Quit with the lip service that "this too shall pass". Yes, it will. And everyone in my circle is tired of my quip that it will pass like a kidney stone. Nothing lasts forever—neither good nor bad. Forget the label and accept what is and start envisioning what you want the other side to look like and envision realistically what the future will look like and plan and work towards it. Some to many of your clients will continue to work from home. How will you work with them? Many of your clients have upped their online game and are researching and buying more and more from the computer. How are you planning for that? Remember—you are the programmer for your future!

First things first. Steven Covey taught us to DO, PLAN, DELEGATE and ELIMINATE by filtering things through a matrix. If it is Urgent and Important—Do it now. If it is Not Urgent but Important—Plan it and schedule it. If it is Not Important but Urgent, what he called distractions with deadlines—Delegate it. Find or hire someone to take care of it. If it's Not Urgent and Not Important—Eliminate it. Get rid of frivolous distractions.

Think Win-Win. Keep in mind that everyone is facing this same storm. It is creating problems on an equal opportunity basis. Value and respect your customers and suppliers by understanding a "win" for everyone is the best resolution. This isn't about being nice. It's about your character and living out genuine feelings for mutually beneficial solutions.

Seek first to understand, then to be understood. Too many of us listen to respond. Put some effort into empathy. You create an atmosphere of caring, positive problem-solving and authenticity by genuinely trying to understand other people. You'll be amazed at how much more creative you'll become as you are now able to see solutions because you understand the problems.

Synergize! Very simply, you've got a great team of people to draw from to get more work done and achieve your goals. Combine the strengths of your supplier partners, reps, your industry community (regional and national associations) and even your clients to build a team and experience positive teamwork that moves mountains.

Sharpen the Saw. Many of us have used this time productively to learn new skills, listen to podcasts and join webinars and learn from the multitude of resources we're so fortunate to have in this wonderful sharing industry of ours. The Japanese call this Kaizen or Continuous Improvement. Balance and renew your health, energy and resources to create and build long-term, effective lifestyles. Focus on physical, mental, spiritual well-being and using service to others allows one to create an upward spiral of renewal.

Integrate these seven principles into your life as you work toward leading yourself to a more effective and successful future.

CHAPTER 22
THEY'RE STILL BUYING, IF YOU OFFER WHAT THEY'RE LOOKING FOR...

CLIENTS AND PROSPECTS are still buying—no matter what the news media is trying to tell you. No matter what your co-workers, competitors or suppliers are saying. Your customers still need you and still want to buy from you.

The thing about this economy is that it clarifies something. They don't want to buy promotional products. And truth be told—they don't want to buy promotional products in a great economy either. What your customers want to buy is a more efficient, more profitable, more exciting company. They want to buy a better brand. They want to buy the ability to be the first choice among shoppers looking for the services and products that they offer. They want to buy loyal customers. They want to buy engaged, committed employees. They want to buy results.

You have a tool kit of three-dimensional media that can be put to use when combined with your creativity and your problem-solving ability to give your customers just what they want, when they want it. They want to buy what you have to sell:

INCREASE
increase return on marketing investments with the one medium that can touch all five senses. Increase engagement and involvement with a medium that touches people where they live and how they live. Increase value by providing a medium that "remains to be seen" and is used over and over again.

MOTIVATION
motivating sales forces to make the extra calls, mail the extra letters, prospect just a little deeper. Motivating customers to read the offer

details, stop in and compare, visit the trade show booth, reactivate an old account. Motivating employees to ask for the add-ons, to take the time to assure complete customer satisfaction.

*P*ROMOTION
to call out the features and benefits of your clients' products and services in a creative and engaging way. To build a brand image and reinforce key messages so that your customers are top of mind, all the time.

*A*PPRECIATION
to customers for stopping by, for taking a test ride, for filling out an application, for joining an email list, for buying a first time, a second time or for on-going loyalty. To employees for going above and beyond, for sacrificing to help out during challenging times, for working more hours for less pay or for working fewer hours to keep fellow workers from being laid off. A little appreciation goes a long way—especially right now.

*R*ECOGNITION
to spread positive emotions and make people feel valued. Recognition among peers and in the community. What gets recognized gets repeated.

*T*RAINING
providing tangible advertising that can reinforce key training messages, be used as a communications device to carry messages, motivate people to learn, remind folks of the lessons learned.

IMPART that kind of thinking and those kinds of services to your clients and they'll buy from you in any economy. Remember I-M-P-A-R-T are six products that you sell that everyone will always need and will always have a budget for. When you sell results—when you sell Increase, Motivation, Promotion, Appreciation, Recognition and Training—you IMPART Value that sets you apart from the competition and allows you not only to survive a tough economy but to Thrive in any economy.

IMPART VALUE

I — INCREASE RETURN ON MARKETING INVESTMENTS WITH THE ONE MEDIUM THAT CAN TOUCH ALL FIVE SENSES.

M — MOTIVATION. MOTIVATING SALES FORCES. MOTIVATING CUSTOMERS. MOTIVATING EMPLOYEES

P — PROMOTION. CALL OUT FEATURES AND BENEFITS. BUILD BRAND IMAGE. REINFORCE KEY MESSAGES.

A — APPRECIATION. THANK CUSTOMERS FOR SHOPPING. THANK EMPLOYEES FOR GOING ABOVE AND BEYOND.

R — RECOGNITION. MAKING PEOPLE FEEL VALUED. WHAT GETS RECOGNIZED GETS REPEATED.

T — TRAINING. TANGIBLE ADVERTISING THAT CAN REINFORCE THE NEW SKILLS AND KNOWLEDGE LEARNED.

"IMPART value that sets you apart from the competition."

CHAPTER 23
THINGS ARE CHANGING. WHETHER FOR THE GOOD OR THE BAD IS YOUR DECISION.

IT IS INCREDIBLY obvious that our lives have changed, and we will evermore view our lives through a lens of before 2020 and after the pandemic. It becomes so simple for us judge the disorder brought to our lives as "bad".

Perhaps a better response is "maybe". By refusing to place a judgement on these events, we can open ourselves to discover the "good" in the events and the opportunities that these events may bring us. We must realize that growth is not always comfortable. Imagine a plant pushing through the ground or the opening of a bud. Opening and blossoming and transitioning requires that we push, move and struggle against the old us in order to discover the newness and beauty it can bring.

We're going to be looking at severely cut budgets. This means that you can be looking for ways to help your clients get better results and more lasting value for each dollar they spend. Promotional products can do that. Your medium has the ability to deliver more impressions for their dollar because it is useful and long-lasting.

We're looking at staffing cuts which means your clients are going to have more responsibilities and a higher need for trusted professionals to partner with to help them get their job done. You have time right now to be increasing your knowledge and professionalism. You can be using all the tools at your disposal to position yourself and your services as the partner who makes their job easier. This is the ideal time for you to develop and implement that Marketing Plan that has been on your To-Do List since Bush (either one) was president.

We'll be seeing a lot less personal face-to-face contact which means that you should be making yourself memorable. Remember, it's not your clients' job to remember you. It's your job to be unforgettable. Be real. Be authentic and be truly and fully committed to solving your clients' problems. Be proactive. Suggest solutions for their upcoming problems and events.

I never tire of reminding you. "Problem Solvers ALWAYS Make Money." If you are not solving problems, you won't make money. And if you're not making money, you are not solving problems!

What other problems are your customers facing and how can you solve them? You should be asking yourself this question all of the time.

They are looking for results. They want to make sure that they are getting maximum Return on Investment, Return on Objectives and Return on Effort. In other words, they want to feel like they made a decision that they are proud of. Make sure you're recommending solutions that make them feel creative, smart, and talented.

They are looking for increasing Positive Emotions. That can mean a lot of things but their stakeholders—employees, customers, suppliers and business partners need to feel appreciated, important, valued and yes, loved. You are fortunate to work in an industry that has about a million ways to make that happen.

They are looking for Positive Experiences. This goes hand in hand with positive emotions. Whether they just hosted a Virtual Gathering or a responsible masked and gloved and socially-distanced event—you need to be coming up with ways to make these memorable, enjoyable and positive.

Like you and me, they are looking for Human Connection. Offer personalized solutions. Find ideas that connect with the things that make others feel good and feel recognized as individuals. Acknowledge and validate the variety of new feelings and emotions that are right there in front of us.

We live in a time of uncertainty and degrees of fear. Be honest. Be authentic. Acknowledge and respect others and other points of view. Be the solution provider that your clients trust to serve the greater good.

There is a story of a wise person who won an expensive car in a sweepstakes. His family and friends were happy for him and said, "You are so lucky!" He smiled and replied, "Maybe." One day a drunken driver crashed into him in his new car and sent him to the hospital. "Wow, this is horrible" all of his friends said. "Maybe" he replied. While in the hospital, a tornado ripped through his town and demolished his house. His friends all exclaimed about how lucky he was that he was in the hospital and not in his home at the time. Again, he said, "Maybe."

Instead of judging the events in his life, he chose instead to accept them. We should also learn to accept this "New Normal". Not as good or bad but for the reality that it is. It is here. We can learn and grow from it and search for opportunity or we can wallow and be sad and blame life, others and fortune.

Choose to grab this moment and let it define you as an innovator and a problem solver. It will be tough work, but it will have its rewards.

CHAPTER 24
5 MINDSET ADJUSTMENTS YOU NEED TO MAKE NOW!

STOP SITTING THERE waiting for things to return to "normal". Normal doesn't exist anymore. It's time for you to start writing your next chapter, planning your next moves, and start making those moves. Here are five mindset adjustments you need to make today to get back on your path to success.

Face it. It's time to be brutally honest with yourself. Recognize that things are not right—right at this very moment. The plans you made in January aren't really relevant anymore. Accept that and get ready to move on.

Find and focus on solutions. Your customers and your prospects have the same problems that you have right now. As you start new habits and daily activities to build relationships while socially distanced, think about how you can apply what you're learning to help your clients solve these same problems.

Put yourself out there and pull yourself back up. This requires courage, strength and endurance. Don't be afraid to stumble, fall or get knocked down. Just be resolved to always get back up. Get very clear on your vision and start working on it. Now.

Avoid excuses. Put your heart into it and pursue it. Life gives the test first and then the lesson. Amaze yourself with your own determination and can-do spirit. Don't be afraid to be passionate about helping others rise.

Just Do It! (apologies to Nike). Rise up and realize the blessings of the dark night and the potential of the new day. There will be a time when you'll look back at 2020. Make your future self proud of how you handled it. Starting now.

With your constant commitment to make daily improvements and create positive habits, and a heart for helping others you will discover opportunities that you never dreamed of before and have the chance to make them your new reality.

To RISE requires Resilience, Inspiration, Service and Excellence. Build these attributes into your day and get ready to thrive.

"Every organization must be prepared to abandon <u>everything</u> it does to survive in the future."

—PETER DRUCKER

CHAPTER 25
COVID-19. THIS TOO IS A DEFINING MOMENT

WHEN WE SPEAK and write about generational themes, we often reference shared major moments in life that define a generation. For the generation prior to Baby Boomers, it was Pearl Harbor and World War II. Many Baby Boomers can describe where they were and what they were doing when JFK was assassinated. For Gen Xers, the Shuttle Challenger disaster is a singular moment and Millennials were shaped by the events of September 11, 2001. For Gen Z, the Great Recession of 2008 disrupted family life in their formative years. Many have asked what will the new Generation be named—the one who follows X, Y (Millennials) and Z? Already, demographers are labeling the youngest among us as Gen C for Coronavirus.

We should remind however, the events mentioned above in the context of understanding generations have profound impact on everyone. The experience we are all sharing right now of a worldwide pandemic shutting down our worlds and creating havoc with our businesses is a Defining Moment for all of us.

There was a time when multiple disappointments and setbacks totally upended my life and my plans. Within a six-month period, a best friend died suddenly, a business partner committed suicide, and my marriage disintegrated. At a most shocking moment of betrayal, anger and hurt, I called a friend out of desperation and received life-changing advice. "Paul, he said, "you are experiencing a Defining Moment. What you decide to do with it may determine your future."

Because of this advice, I was able to make value-based decisions that did indeed allow me to choose love over hate, victory over victimhood and clarity to see opportunities that opened up in front of me.

As this pandemic rages through our country and the world and our businesses dry up and loved ones get sick and we cannot see the end or a way out it is time to remember that "This Too Shall Pass." There is another side and a way out. We may not know what the future holds but we do know that nothing succeeds like resilience. Getting knocked down doesn't matter as long as you just keep on getting up. If you need a moment to wallow or to mourn the past, take it and then get back up and move on.

This perfect defining moment is going to be very uncomfortable. We seem pretty hardwired to not like change. But growth requires change. Trust this moment and live here. No one can go back and change the past. So, let go of the shoulda's. The past does not exist.

Don't worry about the future. Plan for it yes. React in the present moment with today's reality and don't write fantasies about how bad it's going to be. The future is fantasy. It is not real. This moment is the only reality and right now, you have what you need in the now.

Acceptance of my present experience did not come easily or comfortably but two teachers appeared with words I could own. Eckhart Tolle in *"A New Earth"* wrote, "Life will give you whatever experience is most helpful for the evolution of your consciousness. How do you know this is the experience you need? Because this is the experience you are having at this moment." And Byron Katie reinforced that thought with the instruction to "Love What Is." It is the only reality you have so you can love it or suffer. The only two choices.

The pandemic and accompanying economic downturn are our reality. How we decide to think about it and act through it is our personal story. Write a good one.

April and I climbed 103 stories to the observation deck of Willis Tower (formerly known as Sears Tower) in Chicago.

FIND YOUR FOCUS

 FIRST THINGS FIRST

 OBJECTIVES

 CONSISTENCY

 UNDERSTAND

 SINGLE TASKING

"Five tips to improve your productivity and results by finding your FOCUS"

CHAPTER 26
FIND YOUR FOCUS

You are constantly being distracted. Your phone dings and off you go. Your email alert sounds and down another rabbit hole you go. We keep finding more and more ways to receive information but rarely think about our why or what we should be doing with it. It seems that all of these new productivity tools can actually hurt our productivity. So here are five tips to improve your productivity and results by finding your FOCUS.

F
   First Things First Stephen Covey wrote a book by that title with the challenge to get us to think about things in four quadrants: 1) Important and Urgent; 2. Important, Not Urgent; 3. Urgent, Not Important and 4. Not Urgent, Not Important. Determine what is most important and most urgent and take care of those tasks first. Learn to stay out of number 3 and number 4 until your Important Tasks are completed.

O
   Objectives. Do you know your goals? Did you set any goals for this year, this quarter, this month, this week, this day? An amazing number of us go through life without taking the time to write our future. You write your future by setting your specific, measurable, achievable, relevant and time-bound goals. As the Cheshire Cat told Alice, "If you don't know where you're going, any road will take you there."

C
   Consistency. The only road to success is to make success a habit. The only way to create a habit is to do the right thing every day and every time. This meets the #1 test of Urgent and Important. If you're serious

about doing more and getting more from your life, you must be consistent. For me this has meant to put important self-improvement activities on my calendar. Make an appointment with yourself to plan, to meditate, to think, to strategize and to do the important things first.

U

Understand. Understand yourself. Understand your own little habits that undermine your efforts. Understand your why. When you know why you're doing what you do, it makes the road clearer, decisions easier and helps you stay on course. You free yourself to be your best self and to live out the unique you. You'll get comfortable and that is attractive because you are more real. And people like working with people who are real.

S

Single-Tasking. Too many of us like to brag about our ability to multi-task. It's not something to be particularly proud of. Prioritize your list of tasks and then knock them off one-by-one. There's not much that is more satisfying than a piece of paper with multiple tasks marked as complete—one by one by one. Turn off all distractions and get each one done.

CHAPTER 27
QUIT TRYING TO BE EVERYTHING TO EVERYONE.

Ever think about how much more you could accomplish if you would focus on less?

Get out of the idea that you can do it all and get really good at just a few things. Be very mindful of what you want your business to look like.

Decide who you want to work with and get very conscientious about only pursuing the types of people and companies that will allow you to do your very best work. Just because someone can buy promotional products doesn't mean you should be selling to them. If you want a relationship and they want a transaction—guess what?—it won't fit. If they want to solve a problem and you want to make a quick sale—guess what?—it won't fit. Get clear about what your ideal customer looks like and pursue them. The opposite is also as true. Get clear about who your worst nightmare is and run the other way.

Know what you like to sell and get really, really good at that category. Learn the full range of opportunities and solutions that the product category can offer and become the expert. Clients like to know they are dealing with professionals and experts in their field. With the hundreds of product categories and nearly million products available in our industry, you can't possibly be an expert in all of them.

Pick a lane and stay there. I don't believe that in more than thirty years of selling promotional products that I ever—and I mean ever!—tried to start a relationship by telling a prospect that I sold promotional products. I targeted large accounts and began the conversation talking about my experience in creating sales promotion programs and incentive programs to motivate the sales force, dealers and consumers. What's your lane? What problem do you solve?

Keep learning. When you've narrowed down who you want to work with, what you want to help people with and what problems you can solve—you can focus your professional development to the seminars, webinars, blogs and articles that will help you become a true expert. You'll have a whole lot of less in your brain and become a focused subject matter expert who builds relationships and builds a satisfying career.

CHAPTER 28
ARE YOU BETTER THAN YOU WERE YESTERDAY?

YESTERDAY'S INNOVATION IS today's expectation. The great new value-added service you added is now expected of you. With every interaction with your clients, you need to be thinking about how you can make them feel great.

In an August 2011 Forbes article, author Marc Compeau wrote about the Satisfaction Formula, a concept that innovative Dave Sweet has built a ten-tactic program called S.E.R.V.E. F.I.R.S.T. He and his daughter Jayna Sweet published *The Satistaction Formula: A Multi-Generational Strategy To Maximize Customer Engagement*. The formula states that satisfaction can be measured by taking the Experience Minus the Expectation and come up with a positive or negative number.

Last weekend, my wife and I had a high value gift certificate for a very high end, award-winning restaurant. We planned our evening around the experience and can state that our Expectation was for a 10 Experience. Instead, we received the worst service ever on almost every conceivable level. So, our Experience was a One. One Minus Ten Equals Minus Nine. (It was the type of bad experience that ends up on Yelp—yes, this one did—and with us telling others and naming names). A negative number that high means there is little they can do to ever win us back. I'm not sure if they gave us another $150.00 gift certificate that we would even give them a second chance.

Think of the reverse of that situation though. Have you ever gone into an experience with pretty low expectations only to have them blown away? A high positive number also sends you to Yelp and to telling friends and anyone who will listen only with a positive intent.

I'm not telling you that you should shoot for delivering high positive numbers. But I am telling you that you should consistently deliver at least a Plus One. (The reason you don't want to always deliver a high plus experience is because it becomes unsustainable as your customers' expectations can become so high as to make it impossible for you to reach them.

Here's the point. ***BE JUST A LITTLE BIT BETTER EACH TIME***. Maybe smile a little wider. Listen a little closer. Be conscious of your words and attitude. Make them feel like your most important client. Because in that moment, they are.

CHAPTER 29
IF YOU DON'T KNOW, HOW WILL THEY KNOW?

How does what you do help your customer feel smarter, better, more savvy and just plain good? Have you ever thought deeply and clearly about your value proposition so that you can clearly explain it?

Your value proposition is how you and your solution help your customers win. How you make a meaningful difference to their business and it describes how you are different from your competition.

Knowing how you make a difference while being different can position you to take price out of the buyer's equation. It opens doors for you. Visualize the results you provide and then use that language so your clients and prospects can recognize it and value it.

What's in it for me? is the number one question on everyone's mind. Your customers are not thinking, "I wonder what s/he can sell me today?"

They want to know what problem you can solve for them.

They want to feel smart, strategic, creative and productive.

They only care about how you can solve their pain or bring them success.

Think about your successes. Ask your best customers what they feel when they work with you. Use your past success to build your future successes.

Become a storyteller with compelling stories about how you "find the pain and are the aspirin" for what ails their organization.

Your stories, you value proposition move you toward your purpose and working from your passion.

"Prescription
without
Diagnosis
is
Malpractice."

CHAPTER 30
TO INCREASE YOUR SALES—QUIT SELLING

How is it that nobody likes to be sold to, but everyone loves to buy? Can you sell to someone who instinctively hates being sold? The most successful professionals have stopped selling and instead work to be trusted advisors to their clients.

Be a Mindful Servant and watch how more satisfying your career becomes and how loyalty among your customers soars. What if you went to a doctor who immediately laid out a tray full of prescription drugs and started extolling the virtues of each and why you should buy them? You would think the physician was a hopeless kook!

Instead take a page from all professionals. Ask questions to understand your customer, who they are, what they want to achieve, where they are coming from. After trying many years to get an appointment with a major pharmaceutical company, I arrived at my first appointment with just a padfolio and pen. The buyer was astounded. "Where's your suitcase?" he asked. "Suitcase?" I responded. "Yes, all of the trinket salespeople come to my office with a suitcase and start putting all sorts of stuff on my desk" he answered. I said, "I came here to learn about your business and needs today and then I'll come back if I have some solutions for you. I have found that prescription without diagnosis is malpractice."

By the way, I enjoyed several years of six and seven figure business from that buyer after I understood their needs. The foundation of any relationship and especially a consultative relationship is TRUST. Clients will not buy from you until they trust you and to earn that trust, put your needs aside and focus laser-like on their needs. You can't bring them value unless you understand what they value.

Your clients don't buy things—they buy avoidance of pain or pursuit of pleasure. You must know what they consider painful, where they've been and where they're going in order to become a compelling partner and trusted team member.

"Prescription without diagnosis is malpractice."

"Clients will not buy from you until they trust you and to earn that trust, put your needs aside and focus laser-like on their needs."

SUMMIT
REACHING THE PEAK OF YOUR POTENTIAL

Part 4: 10 Differentiation Strategies

CHAPTER 31: HOW ARE YOU DIFFERENT?

CHAPTER 32: WHAT PROBLEM DO YOU SOLVE?

CHAPTER 33: CREATE A BRAND YOU!

CHAPTER 34: FIVE SMART WAYS TO GROW YOUR BUSINESS.

CHAPTER 35: TAKE IT UP TO THE NEXT LEVEL

CHAPTER 36: WHY SHOULD THEY CHOOSE YOU?

CHAPTER 37: HOW DID YOU BECOME A COMMODITY?

CHAPTER 38: THE ONLY MARKETING YOU NEED

CHAPTER 39: BEFORE AND AFTER

CHAPTER 40: BUT HOW CAN YOU BE DIFFERENT?

"Come up with five points of difference between you and your competitors."

CHAPTER 31
HOW ARE YOU DIFFERENT?

CAN YOU COME up with **FIVE POINTS** where your customers would regard you or your organization as being different from everything else, they see in the marketplace? Can you come up with three? One?

Being different is a competitive advantage in the new economy. It is critical that you be able to stand out from the crowd. Who are your competitors? Have you looked at their website, their brochure, their marketing efforts? How does your marketing differ and stand out?

Having friendly service, being able to source products, being responsive and able to provide quotes and proposals quickly, having competitive pricing—these are requirements in today's economy. Those are the cost of entry. Can you really differentiate yourself along these claims?

You may need to reinvent yourself or your company along several lines. Peter Drucker said, "Every organization must be prepared to abandon *everything* it does to survive in the future." Are you prepared?

Unless you can differentiate yourself from your competition, you WILL be caught into that zero-sum game of commoditization, where the race to the bottom becomes a vicious cycle of more and more work, frustration, stress and anxiety and less and less profit and joy. All of the reasons that you came into this business are lost when you get caught up in that game.

Seth Godin has put it best. "Be Better. Be Different. Or Be Cheaper." One of the best ways to be better and different is to have a relentless pursuit of continuous improvement, creative problem solving and focus on customer needs.

Here's my challenge to you. Take a week and work on this. Discuss it with your employees, with your customers, with your suppliers, with your mastermind group. Come up with five points of difference between you and your competitors that everyone will agree defines you. Then communicate those points of difference.

Appreciate
Recognize
Motivate
Promote
Instruct
Train

CHAPTER 32
WHAT PROBLEM DO YOU SOLVE?

WHAT IS THE problem that you solve? Quick. You have seven seconds. If you can't tell someone in seven seconds what you can do for them, you probably won't sell them. They don't want to know what you sell. They don't want to know your mission statement, vision statement, value statement or bank statement. WIIFM? What's in it for me? What problem of mine can you solve? Tell me. Quick.

We have all talked about, crafted and perfected our "elevator speech." Forget it. You don't have thirty seconds. You have seven. If you don't have any problems to solve, you're not in the game. And you want to be in the game, don't you? Finding a promotional product is not a big-time problem. I don't know of any buyers today who don't know how to use a computer, who don't know how to find a web browser, who haven't heard about Google.

Not many clients have a promotional products problem. So, what is the problem that you solve? Problem solvers ALWAYS make money. Clients do have problems with worker productivity, with declining profits, with people performance, with their brand or business presence. Can you help them solve productivity, profit, performance or presence problems? Clients have problems with people—attracting the best, training them and retaining the good ones. They need to communicate their purpose. Do you have the tools to help them solve those problems?

You may need to look long and hard to find a customer looking for promotional products, but do you know of any business that is not wanting to increase sales, lower their costs, keep their current customers happy, reactivate old customers and motivate and inspire everyone they touch? You've got a toolbox of solutions for those problems.

What problem do you solve? I solve ARMPIT problems. I help companies Appreciate, Recognize, Motivate, Promote, Instruct, Train. Now, can I say that in seven seconds?

In any economy, problem solvers create value and make money. Find the pain. Be the Aspirin. You can create prosperity. But you need to start. Now.

CHAPTER 33
CREATE A BRAND YOU!

IF YOU COULD make $1.00 per hour, $4.00 per hour, $40.00 per hour, $160.00 per hour or $600.00 per hour; which would choose? If you're still in the business of selling product to buyers, you're choosing the low end of the spectrum. If you're in the business of creating experiences for your clients, you can aspire to and achieve the top end. If you're focused on how to be the lowest priced company, you're working hard to commoditize yourself and are engaged in a zero-sum game.

Nearly everything that can be raised, mined, harvested or slaughtered starts out its life as a commodity. And those who try to strip out costs and services are guilty of playing the price game rather than raising and creating value. Commodities are sold by traders and bought by markets and was the characteristic of the agrarian society.

When commodities get standardized, packaged, processed and inventories the value moves up as goods are born. Typically sold by manufacturers and bought by users, goods are typical of the industrial age. Many great brands were born in this age as marketers defined the unique selling proposition and stable easily defined markets behaved predictably and could be reached through mass media.

Most of us in the promotional products business are service providers—both suppliers and promotional consultants alike. We've moved up to the third level of value and are part and parcel of the Service Economy. As providers, we customize our offerings for our clients who benefit from us doing the things that they just don't want to do themselves. There's a lot of competition in this space with most of the price concessions coming from the value we put on our own good service and intellectual property.

But the sweet spot and the fourth and fifth or more level of value come when we can move ourselves into becoming Experience Stagers. In today's economy our audiences or guest want sensation. They want meaning. They want value. These are intangibles that innovative, creative people can make happen if we learn to not just sell promotions, but to stage experiences. Welcome to the Experience Economy. This is a place where right brain thinkers, where creativity, where meaning and values rules. And people are willing to pay the price—your price—for your unique blend of Brand YOU.

In order to raise your game, increase your value and your profit potential, you need to escalate your performance in two areas—competitive position and your relevancy to the needs of your customers.

How can you differentiate yourself from your competition? What are your unique skills, ideas, personal strengths, core values and mission that make you the only game in town? Find them and work them.

And how can you be more relevant to the needs of your customers? How can you become a part of their business? What things are they doing that you can do better and more efficiently? What ideas can you generate proactively that will create a sense of team and partnership? Can you customize your offerings so that you become an extension of your clients' organizations? How can you make them feel? If your answer to that question is that you can make them feel that they got the best price, you've opened the door for anyone who can give them the same feeling.

Your life work should allow you to become the best you possible. To reach your best potential, you need to live out your values with passion and commitment. Your clients will feel it. They'll know it and appreciate it. Change the game. Instead of looking for what can be cut, focus on the value that can be created. Get in the business of creating results, meaning, engagement, relationships and experiences.

Welcome to the Experience Economy! Welcome to Brand You.

CHAPTER 34
5 SMART WAYS TO GROW YOUR BUSINESS

How do you step up and begin moving your business to better results? Well first of all you need to make some changes. That means taking a couple steps to the edge of your comfort zone and sometimes going right out there to the edge. Growth requires change. That's why it's called growth.

NUMBER ONE.

You need to spend more time on money making activities. If you're not prospecting, contacting, meeting with clients or creating sales opportunities, you are not going to get more sales. Set an alarm on your smartphone to go off at random times throughout the day and make a note of what you are doing at that moment. Is it the $100.00 per hour work or the $10.00 per hour work? What you are doing will determine how much you're going to make.

NUMBER TWO.

Move your least profitable accounts to others. If you have salespeople or a sales assistant, reassign the bottom of our account list to them. This can be the most effective way for you to grow. Those accounts will get better service from someone else and you'll be able to spend your time on your most profitable accounts and your big hairy audacious dream account list.

NUMBER THREE.

Prospect for bigger fish. You do have big, hairy, audacious dream accounts, don't you? In my career, I was able to work with huge accounts because I was either brave enough or stupid enough to call on them, to research them, to provide ideas for them. One major account took me nineteen years to land but it became a seven figure per year account for me. I believe you should have ten big dreams that you are working on at all times.

NUMBER FOUR.
Create a STOP DOING LIST! Everyone likes to brag about their long to-do lists. Having a Stop-Doing-List can be much more profitable. You need to stop doing the things that are not paying off. Activity may make you feel better but unless it's getting profitable results for you, it's time to stop it now. See number one above.

NUMBER FIVE.
Increase your average order size. If you've moved your accounts that are doing small orders to others and you've begun prospecting for bigger fish, you have a good start on this. Become a specialist in higher end and higher ticket items. Sell programs and sell into programs such as wellness, trade shows and other areas where you can get bigger orders. It takes the same amount of overhead, same amount of effort and the same amount of time to sell a small order as it does a giant sized one. Make it worth your while.

If you follow these five steps, you'll be setting yourself up to grow. But you need to stay disciplined, you need to risk turning over small accounts so that you have time to develop bigger ones and you need the courage to go after your dreams. Dream Big.

CHAPTER 35
TAKE IT TO THE NEXT LEVEL.

To what lengths will you go to make yourself remarkable to your clients? If you're not willing to think harder, research more, and care more than your competition, guess what? You lose!

Why should a customer change their relationship, change their habits and take a risk to work with you? Because you can get a better price? Really? Is that the kind of customer you want? If they'll change to you for a nickel, they'll drop you for a nickel.

The only way to turn customers into fans is to be deserving. The only way to be deserving is to make such a remarkable impression and give them something new. Somewhere along the way, you'll have to make a heart connection. You'll need to change how they feel.

To take it to the next level, you need to know why you want that relationship. If you're just seeking a transaction, both of you will know it. When you get genuinely interested in your customers problems and have a strong desire to help them solve those problems, they'll know that as well.

When your customers know that you are excited about helping and not just excited about making a sale, they'll be ready to move with you to the next level. You need to learn what your customers want to create, accomplish, feel or have. You need to understand and be able to articulate their challenges. When they know that they are the reason that you get up in the morning and that thinking about their problems really juice you—they will feel it and they will want what you have to offer.

Take it to the next level and offer them your heart, your passion, your art and your best. Help them be a better version of themselves when they work with you.

1. Who is Your Customer?
2. What Does Your Customer Need?
3. What Do You Deliver?
4. How Do You Deliver Your Promise?
5. How is That Different from the Competition?
6. What do you Offer that the Competition Cannot Touch?

CHAPTER 36
WHY SHOULD THEY CHOOSE YOU?

If you don't know why customers should choose to work with you over all of their other options, how in the world are they ever going to know? You need to know the answer to that and be able to articulate it, believe in it and live it. Here are six questions you need to answer and how to put those answers together to create your Value Proposition.

1. Who is Your Customer? You will be able to find your customers easier when you have defined what they look like, what they believe in, what values they share with you in common and how they behave. What adjectives do you use to describe your best customers? Open-minded? Fun-loving? Metrics-driven? Value-oriented? Price-savvy? Come up with your description.

2. What does Your Customer Need? Does your customer need a complete concept to completion assistant? Do they need fresh ideas or are they simply looking for someone who can get them what they demand? Do they need lots of options? Do they need program expertise, help defining and measuring results? Do they need a lot of customer service, support and handholding? What descriptive nouns can you use to describe what they need? Great ideas? Accurate delivery? Sweet design?

3. What Do You Deliver? What is it that you deliver for your customers? What can they expect to receive from you? How is it different from anything else they can find in the marketplace? Can you be more exciting and different than just saying you deliver good quality at a good price? Work at this

one because it is important that you know what it is that you are going to be able to deliver to your customers every time.

4. How do you deliver what you just promised above? For example, if I promise that I deliver fresh, exciting ways for my clients to grow their business, I need to be able to say HOW I'm going to do that. It might be by being an award-winning creative who has worked on top national brands. It might be because you have more industry experience, or because you were a former buyer yourself.

5. How is What You Do and How You Do It Different than the Competition? I know we all have been told to not badmouth the competition. That advice is sound. Don't name a specific competitor but do know how you are better than your competition? Many of us complain about certain online competitors and lament how they can beat us on price. Come on. Work harder than that. If you're going to compete with the internet, make yourself more valuable and more interesting than a website for goodness sakes. How are you better and different? Is your competition stale? Does it care about product safety? Does it go the extra mile? Does it offer a real person at all times?

6. What do you offer that the competition just can't touch? Say it loud and say it proud. What makes you unique? What makes you the best and only choice for the type of customer who has the type of need that you can solve and amaze while doing it?

Now put it all together. For **DESCRIBE YOUR CUSTOMER** (#1) needing **DESCRIBE YOUR CUSTOMER'S PAIN POINT** (#2), I deliver **INPUT YOUR ANSWER TO NUMBER 3 ABOVE**, and I do this by **INPUT YOUR ANSWER FROM NUMBER 4 ABOVE**; unlike my competition which **DESCRIBE HOW WHAT DO AND HOW YOU DO IT IS DIFFERENT THAN YOUR COMPETITION** (#5), I offer **DESCRIBE YOUR UNIQUE OFFERING** (#6).

There. You have it. Your very own Value Proposition. Here is what one might look like:

For **THE VALUE CONSCIOUS, MARKETING-SAVVY CUSTOMER** needing **SALES PROMOTIONS THAT GET RESULTS**, my company delivers **THE NEWEST, TRENDIEST AND MOST BUZZ-WORTHY PROMOTION IDEAS** and does this by **STAYING CURRENT WITH NEW OPPORTUNITIES WHILE BEING GROUNDED IN OVER TWO DECADES OF SUCCESSFUL PROMOTION PLANNING**, unlike the competition which **RISE AND FALL QUICKLY AND DEPEND ON ME-TOO AND WASHED-UP TRENDS**. I offer **A FRESH APPROACH THAT GENERATES NOT ONLY BUZZ BUT CREATES RESULTS**.

You will be amazed by how working through this exercise can help you articulate your value proposition and make it real.

CHAPTER 37
HOW DID YOU BECOME A COMMODITY?

How in the world did you allow yourself to become a commodity? When did this happen?

The snarky answer? Because you allowed it. You chased after it. You encouraged it. The need to make a sale overcame your need to make a living, to build a brand.

What is a Commodity? A commodity is a product that is exactly like another product. They are easy to find in the promotional products business where we often sell the same products from the same suppliers to the same customers in the same way.

Commoditization is the process that your buyers followed to reduce their buying decision to the lowest common denominator—price.

It happens when you have not found consistently effective ways to connect your unique value to the client's business and personal emotions. It happens when you don't make sure that you are doing the extra things that make you more valuable or even indispensable to your customers.

It is exacerbated by competitors who are more and more becoming practitioners of commoditization themselves. Distributors who spend extra hours looking for another supplier who will sell them something for a nickel cheaper. Distributors who will go direct to unproven, unknown manufacturers outside of the industry channels to save a few pennies.

And oh, the irony. These are the ones we hear bemoaning the "disloyal" customer who shopped them and gave their business to someone else to save a nickel.

Guess what? The customer who buys from you on price will leave you on price.

Two suggestions. First, quit being a commodity buyer yourself and develop true partnerships with your best suppliers and demonstrate the loyalty that you want to receive from your clients. Second, always put yourself in your client's shoes. Think like them. Speak in terms of their needs, their wants and their highest aspirations. Make them feel smart, professional, safe, secure and understood.

Instead of joining in the race to the bottom and playing the "how low can you go" game, focus on reinventing yourself. Differentiate. Specialize. Deliver something that the client can't easily get elsewhere. That may require extra learning, extra research and extra work on your part. But instead of spending your time looking for a cheaper supplier, spend that time figuring out how you can become an invaluable part of your client's team.

Move up the value ladder. A product commands a higher value when it becomes a good. Cans of branded coffee are priced four hundred times higher than bags of coffee beans. Make sure you differentiate and that you know who you are and what business you are in.

Commodities place you in a race to the bottom. It's a race you do not want to win.

CHAPTER 38
THE ONLY MARKETING YOU NEED

Astound me! That's right knock my socks off! Make me notice that you are different!

Make me talk about you—positively. Make me want to brag about you.

The only marketing you need to always be amazing. If you do that, your customers will share you with people they like. They will want to be the hero who brought you to their friends' attention.

How do you get to be amazing? It takes a conscious and conscientious effort. It's intentional. Care to be the best. That's right. Care honestly about your customers. You want to make them look good. You want them to succeed. You want them to get a promotion. Care. And be the best.

What if? What if your customer or prospective client was paying you to call on them? Would you prepare differently if they were paying you $250.00 for your presentation?

It is costing you at least that much to make that call. So why aren't you preparing, presenting and rehearsing so that you are giving them that level of care and professionalism every time you call on them.

When you are intentional and mindful on every interaction with your clients, you are setting yourself up to be the very best version of yourself.

When your customers think about you, what do they think? One time I was walking down a hallway with a client when a sales person greeted him enthusiastically. As the client and I continued down the hallway, the client muttered, "That guy is always trying to sell me coffee mug." In other words, this ad specialty salesman had become "The Mug Guy." Believe me. You don't want to be the mug guy, the pen gal or the t-shirt person. You want to be the problem solver who always amazes!

Be the best version of yourself and always, ALWAYS give it your best effort. Practice. Rehearse. Research. Work harder than your competition.

When you care to be the best, your customers will see the difference, feel the difference and they will want to share what they found. That is the only marketing you will ever need. Don't fake it till you make. Be the real deal. Live your integrity. Be Amazing!

CHAPTER 39
BEFORE AND AFTER

Answer this. Believe your answer. You will be well on your way to defining your competitive advantage, your value proposition and will become more successful at differentiating yourself and your company. You will be well on your way to moving away from the commodity business and being an innovative value creator.

Describe your client's life *BEFORE* they started working with you. What problems did they face? What were their worries and concerns? What kept them up at night? What fears were they forced to live with as part of their regular work life?

Before you, did they know about the power of promotional products and all of the ways they can be used to solve business problems? Did they know that they could add a person to their staff who is a professional and can make sure every promotion program gets executed flawlessly? Did they know how to make sure their brand would always look great, and all their colors would be perfect? Did they know that they needed to make sure the products were safe and in compliance with safety regulations?

Describe your client's life *AFTER* they became your customer. What problems have you solved for them? How have you made them worry-free? Why do they sleep better? How do they feel more successful and more empowered? Can they imagine going back to life before they discovered what working with a real professional would feel like?

Would they miss you is you left the business? What things do you need to do to make your customers feel that strongly? What are the things you can do for them that your competition has never even thought of doing?

This is not easy. But you don't want to be average. Average is just the best of the worst. It is the just good enough. It is also forgettable.

If you're not making a noticeable, no, a REMARKABLE difference in their work, why should they choose you? It takes more than a low price to make this kind of difference.

Think about the difference—the Before and After Difference—that you can make in a client's life. Then go out there and do it.

"If you're not making a REMARKABLE difference in your clients' work, why should they choose you?"

CHAPTER 40
BUT HOW CAN YOU BE DIFFERENT

But HOW can I be different? You sell the same stuff from the same suppliers to the same people the same way and then you complain that your customers are buying on price. So along I come and tell you to be different. Hah! you say. What does that mean and how can I be different?

You can be different by caring more about solving your customers' problems than you are about making a sale. This might mean recommending a better solution even if it's not something that you can provide to make your client look good. You'll be different by being patient, authentic and truly caring. You'll be different because you'll be trusted.

You can be different by always being professional. You'll always dress the part. You always dress up your presentations. You treat your proposals with respect. You dress them up as well. Even when selling to an admin person, you are ready to present to the CEO. You work hard at personal and professional development and it shows.

You're in it to win it. You are committed to being the best in your professional. Clients do notice the certifications after your name. They notice your volunteer service. They notice that you are respected by your peers. You do the things necessary to earn that respect.

You realize that each interaction is an opportunity. We've all read about how much it costs to make a sales call but tend to let that slide by our consciousness as just our job. Think about it a little differently. What if your customer was paying you two hundred dollars to call on her? What would you do differently? Would you dress differently? Would you prepare differently? Would you rehearse and practice?

Be different.
Think different.
Speak different.

Your reward will be trust, respect and loyalty.
Those are hard to shop.

SUMMIT
REACHING THE PEAK OF YOUR POTENTIAL

Part 5: Success From The Inside Out

CHAPTER 41: IT'S NOT YOUR CUSTOMER'S JOB TO REMEMBER YOU

CHAPTER 42: DO YOU CARE ENOUGH?

CHAPTER 43: EACH MOMENT IS A DEFINING MOMENT

CHAPTER 44: MINDFUL PROSPECTING

CHAPTER 45: THE SECRETS OF PROSPECTING

CHAPTER 46: COULD THIS BE LOVE?

CHAPTER 47: THEY WANT TO LOVE YOU

CHAPTER 48: GET THE JOB!

CHAPTER 49: GET REAL

CHAPTER 50: KNOW YOUR CUSTOMER

CHAPTER 41
IT IS NOT YOUR CUSTOMER'S JOB TO REMEMBER YOU

IT'S YOUR JOB to be unforgettable.

What are you doing that is going to make you stand out?

What have you done to make your last interaction with your customers memorable?

Have you given them a lasting impression?

Have you left them wanting more? Of you and what you offer?

What if they had such a great time working with you that they can't wait to find an excuse to work with you again?

Loyalty happens when you give your customers more than a transaction. It happens when the results you deliver include an emotional connection, a sense of relationship, trust and values alignment. It happens when you work harder to get to know them, their business, their frustrations, their challenges and their opportunities.

You learn that by being intentional, by being caring, by being authentic and by being willing to do your homework with no guarantees of an immediate concern. For example, I attended the Kitchen and Bath Show, visited appliance dealers, researched the industry for three years before I landed my first order with one of the top appliance manufacturers in the country. I subscribed to Progressive Grocer magazine for years before landing major consumer packaged goods accounts.

Think about the business partners, suppliers, and brands that you admire and love doing business with. What is it that they do that makes them unforgettable to you?

Learn from them. Model their behaviors.

Many in our industry complain about their online internet-based competition. Seriously? Can a website have more personality than you? Can a website provide a more satisfactory experience than you can?

Work on being unforgettable by being your truest and most authentic self. Be willing to risk putting yourself out there and making sweet promotional memories.

> *"It is not your customer's job to remember you. It's your job to be unforgettable."*

CHAPTER 42
DO YOU CARE ENOUGH?

If you don't care enough to figure out their pain, why should they care about you?

Are you tired of being shopped? Have your products become just another commodity? Why doesn't "winning the bid" feel like a win? Did you win if you don't feel good about yourself or your client when you get the order?

Do you spend all of your time learning about your products and zero amount of your time learning about your customer? You have got it wrong. Spend more time researching your customers' business, their industry, their challenges and their problems. Then go to work and think about how you can help them.

When you get to the point where you know what they want to do/create/become/feel or have and you understand the challenges that they face—then and only then will you earn their loyalty, their respect and become an integral part of their team.

If you don't know why they should choose you, they're not going to know either. If all you do is source product, you better be able to find enough customers who don't know how to use the internet, don't have your competitors calling on them and consider that a major challenge.

Care enough to spend some time each week reading up about their company history, the industry that they are a part of, and the unique challenges that they face. Care enough to read their industry trade journals to discover who the players are and what issues are making the front cover. Care enough to learn the correct usage of their logo and the correct colors for their branding.

Google is your friend. Get curious about their business. LinkedIn is your friend. Discover who works there and get an idea of how the business is structured. When you can speak with your customers about their industry and their unique challenges, they will know you care.

You can't just say that you care more than your competition. You need to be able to demonstrate it. You need to learn how to listen, how to observe and how to understand that you need to make your customers feel like a better version of themselves because you came into their lives.

CHAPTER 43
EACH MOMENT IS A DEFINING MOMENT

It would be his only at bat in this World Series. After sitting in the dugout with a hamstring pull and worn-out knees, with his team down 4-3, with two outs and a team mate on first base, his coach called on him to pinch hit. He was facing Dennis Eckersley, the 45 save relief ace of the winningness team in baseball that year. With a count of 3 balls and 2 strikes, with two outs, in the bottom of the ninth inning of Game 1 of the World Series, Kirk Gibson sent the next pitch into the right field stands and limped around the bases. This Gimp-Off home run gave the Los Angeles Dodgers momentum that they carried all the way to become world champions in four games to one. In the midst of adversity, Kirk Gibson had a defining moment.

The United States looked like it had its first gold in women's team gymnastics wrapped up with a lead over second place Russia, when her teammate fell down on both of her vaults. Then on her first vault, she landed hard, heard a pop and fell. When it came time for her second vault, she needed a nearly perfect score for the U.S. to win gold. But the "pop" was bad. Barely able to walk, let alone sprint down a runway, she summoned up a courage rare in a slight eighteen-year-old. Gritting her teeth, believing that everything for everybody depended on her, Kerri Strug sprinted, flung her body onto the horse, twisted and landed on her one good leg. She got the job done, a solid landing from a nearly perfect vault. Then she collapsed in pain onto her hands and knees. Kerri Strug found strength within herself to give the kind of effort that creates a defining moment.

The week before the championship, the media was wondering if he would play. Could he with that knee? With each round, he seemed to lose power, played a bit safer and played a 277-yard hole like a par four, which for superhuman power hitters like him never happened. By the

72nd hole, it was him, a ball and a hole twelve feet away. Sink it and play another day on the deteriorating knee. Miss it and the United States Golf Open Championship goes to another man, with another story. But for the millions watching him, very few had any doubt where that ball was heading. The fifth round against Rocco Mediate went all eighteen holes—even. Finally, on hole number ninety-one, the improbable challenger succumbed to who by now writers were calling the best athlete on the planet. Tiger Woods won the U.S. Open on one leg. With an injured leg that his doctors ordered him not to play on, he went to his deep well of mental and physical toughness to hear his 14th major title. A title that is usually decided on Father's Day holds special meaning to the young man whose father taught him to play, to win and to be the best. Most pundits call this one the greatest golf tournament ever. In this defining moment, Tiger Woods turned his painful perseverance into an art form. "You keep playing," Woods said. "Whatever it is, you just keep going, keep going forward. You just keep going, and there's no finish line, and you just keep pushing and pushing."

In this economy, faced with more regulations, more legislation, an alphabet soup of chemicals and consumer product safety requirements, a changing marketplace, a new generation of buyers—you are in a position to create your Defining Moment. Anybody can do this business in good times. Now is your moment to shine. This is when you need to just keep pushing, just keep going, just try harder, just think smarter.

CHAPTER 44
MINDFUL PROSPECTING

WHERE AND HOW to find new customers—prospecting—is a "lifeblood" activity for any salesperson or organization. In some of my presentations I ask, "How do you prospect?" And answer, "Always and All Ways!" I think many of us get a little bit over-eager and end up chasing the wrong customers.

In my opinion, there is only one thing worse than No Customers and that is having the Wrong Customers. While No Customers means the stress of worrying about how to pay the rent—Wrong Customers add to that worry with a whole lot of Hoop-Jumping, kissing of the southern end of a northbound prospect and wasted time and effort.

Think about who it is you really want to work with and for. If you already have one great client make a list of the attributes of that client so you know what you're looking for. Your job is to clone your best customer. To that you need to prospect mindful of with whom you wish a long-term relationship.

Tips for Mindful Prospecting:

Know with what companies and what types of people you want to do business. What are their characteristics? What types of problems will you be able to solve with them? What industries will you serve? Pay attention to their demographics as well.

Demand respect. You are a professional offering professional problem-solving and have real answers to help them do business better. You don't need to grovel. You don't need to beg. Know your worth and present your value proposition with confidence.

Earn respect. If you're already wondering if you can do number two above, you may need to start by understanding the medium you have chosen as your profession. You need to be able to articulate what problems you can help with and how prospects can use your services to live a better life. (Yes, really!)

Understand that great clients just don't happen overnight. It can take on average about sixteen touches to start a relationship. (I've had great clients that have taken up to nineteen years to land). Use that time to learn about the prospect's business, industry and toughest challenges. Use that time to craft break-through compelling reasons for them to get to know you. Be Patient.

Earning new clients is like getting a job or starting a career. Prepare like you're preparing for an interview for your dream job. Study the company, the organization chart and know what your objective needs to be for each contact. (Hint: You are not closing a product sale on your first personal contact. More likely, you're selling a first appointment).

Starting a client relationship is like starting a personal one. Prepare to take it slow—to get to know each other and to build TRUST. Show them how you are not just out to get a one-night sale but have a future in mind.

Choose the right customers and mindfully choose those who will become loyal, long-term, profitable and importantly—fun to work with and make both of you feel good.

CHAPTER 45
THE SECRETS OF PROSPECTING

FINDING NEW CUSTOMERS needs to become a conscious, yet automatic skill to assure that you've always got a pipeline of new business coming in. Those of us in sales are unemployed if we don't have someone buying from us. How we prospect will determine how much money we make and how much we enjoy what we are doing.

So HOW does one prospect? And WHEN does one prospect? In a simple phrase...**ALL WAYS AND ALWAYS!** Prospecting can mean reading labels on your favorite foods and products to determine where the company is headquartered. It can mean speeding up to read the address on the door of the eighteen-wheeler with the interesting product graphics on its trailer. It means keeping your eyes wide open and being constantly curious.

The number one top secret of prospecting however is a simple one. Have a plan. Whether you're going hunting, fishing, looking for a date or trying to find your next great client, the rules are the same. You need to have a plan and work the plan and not get distracted or tempted away from your plan. A hunter going after big game who starts shooting at rabbits and squirrels is not going to have much luck bringing home a trophy buck. The bass fisherman who puts a bobber on the line and a worm on the hook may catch a few pan fish but isn't coming home with a lunker.

1. Know what you're looking for! What kinds of clients make your day? Who do you love working with? Profile your current clients by their demographics—age, gender, interests and values. This is a relationship business. Know what your great relationships look like and look for more just like them.

2. Know what you're not looking for! What types of people do

you hate to be around? Why would you want them for customers? Don't waste your time chasing a big budget account that would make your life miserable. If you've been burned by people who don't respect the value you bring, who don't value your ideas, who don't share the same core values that you do—run away from them!

3. What do you love to do? What do you love to talk about? What are you passionate about? If you love—Love—LOVE golf, why not track down the names and contacts of your favorite equipment manufacturer, accessory supplier or resort course? Your passion will shine through in every communication that you have with them. Too far away, you say? Why not position yourself as the expert from afar? Doesn't it drive you crazy when your local client is buying from somebody from 150, 300 miles away or more? If you love a business and want to make them your client—GO FOR IT. Make them one of your BHAGs (Big Hairy Audacious Goals in the words of "Good to Great" author Jim Collins).

Create your plan and work it. Figure out what the ideal clients look like, so you'll know them when you see them. Find people that you love to be around, and your work won't seem like work and you'll be amazed by the opportunities that come your way. Get clear on whom you don't want to work with as well. Much has been made in business about having a "to-do" list. I've learned that it is as important to have a "stop doing" list. And in that vein, become clear about the people that waste your time, steal your ideas or worse steal your soul. There are energy suckers out there and some of them control some pretty tempting budgets. Don't make a deal with the devil. Save your health, your wealth, and your identity by making a conscious decision to focus your efforts where you can make a difference and your clients will value the value you bring. Pick your clients like you pick your stocks. Give yourself the opportunity to live out your values and your mission with companies that share those values and your passions. You'll be happier, make more money and be healthier.

The promotional products business gives you the opportunity to make new friends every day. You can do something different every day. You can solve problems, exercise your creativity, help your clients become more innovative and make a difference in the lives of your co-workers, your suppliers, your clients and their employees or their customers. You get to have an impact. You can live a life of meaning and create meaning for those you touch. Grasp your higher calling and recognize the gift that you have. Then go out and find people to share that gift called YOU with. When you do that, you are no longer a product salesperson. You are a person of value who is creating value by living out your values. And that—THAT—is the secret of prospecting.

CHAPTER 46
COULD THIS BE LOVE?

WHAT IS IT about this industry that catches folk, pulls them in and never lets them go? Could it be love? I know many people who have taken "sabbaticals" from this crazy business, but they always come back. Some goes to work for a family business or accepts an offer too good to refuse and then, a year or two later, there they are—at the Expo, at a regional show—on one side of the aisle or the other.

I call this industry the Hotel California. "You can check out any time you want, but you can never leave." Why is that? Is it Love?

RELATIONSHIPS are a big part of it. We tend to develop deep friendships or at least fairly intense acquaintances. Some relationships run deep, others wide, but many of them long. One of the longest relationships in my life outside of family is a friendship with another distributor from another part of the country. Maybe it's because we find people we can share our challenges with who actually understand. We learn together. We share experiences together. Business partners abound in this business and we all need to have each other's back.

CREATIVITY is often mentioned as this industry allows us a high degree of self-expression and releases our inner artist. There is no shortage of creativity demonstrated as humor either. Some of the funniest people work in this industry and you can take the word "funny" any way you want! We innovate. We create demand. We create results.

FREEDOM to work hard or hardly work. Freedom to choose hours and clients and business partners. We are an independent lot. We love our ability to choose who, when, where, how and why we work. We're free to choose a niche market. Free to work online. Free to allow our work to be an expression of who we are. Freedom to comment and add your reasons to this blog below.

Jim Collins in his seminal book, "Good to Great" describes a hedgehog concept as a sweet spot that facilitates greatness. The hedgehog concept is the convergence of what you are passionate about, what you can be best in the world at, and that you can make money doing it. I think for many of us, that describes this business. I love it when I see someone get passionate not just over a writing instrument or a calendar or any of our number of things but genuinely excited about what it can do for a business or a life.

Yup. It must be love.

CHAPTER 47
THEY WANT TO LOVE YOU

It's easy in sales to fall into a bit of a battle worn mindset. Facing rejection. Getting stood-up. Being misunderstood. Getting taken advantage of. Being shopped. Making the sale and then not getting paid, or paid way beyond terms. It's amazing that more of our number don't suffer from Post-Traumatic Stress Disorders (PTSD). Or maybe we do.

Yes, despite that. Keep this in mind. The people who buy from you actually want to fall in love with you and your brand. Customer experience is everything. Every Time.

No one says yes to you and then secretly hopes that you'll disappoint them and fail miserably. Their job, their status, their emotions are on the line too.

It's your job to give them lots of reasons to fall head over heels in love with you, your company, your job and what you deliver for them. Yes. That's your job.

The feelings, the emotions your customer has when you have delivered your promises is what in the end is your differentiating advantage.

They want to Love You. It's your job to make sure that they do!

They will fall in love with Authentic you. Show your genuine humanity. They don't expect you to be perfect. But they do expect you to admit when you make a mistake. They expect you to own problems.

They fall in love with people who make them look good. Give them credit for choosing wisely, for being creative (even if it was your original idea). They want to look good to their peers and their bosses. They love you for helping them do just that.

They fall in love with your transparency. When a project has the potential to go south, be upfront. When problems occur, keep them informed. But have your plans ready. Hope for the original but have Plan B in your pocket and Plan C on your desk.

Your clients want a lasting relationship. One that they can depend on with a person they can trust. Yes. They want to love you. Be loveable.

CHAPTER 48
GET THE JOB!

Do You Want That Job?
If you want to become a part of your clients' team and you want to become more than a vendor, change your approach. Quit being a salesperson and become a key employee.

How do you do that? You change your mindset. Think about how you would go about getting a job at your prospect's company. If you want to land a key marketing job at a Fortune 100 company, you will do things differently than if you just want to sell some stuff to them. That's what I'm suggesting.

Determine if this is the type of company that you want to work for. Would you apply to work for a company with a reputation for taking advantage of their employees and treating them badly? If not, why would you want to work for a company that doesn't show respect to their people or their suppliers.

Learn everything you can about the company. You can do this online with search engines. You can set up Google Alerts to keep up to date with news about the company. You can subscribe to their trade magazines and attend one of their industry trade shows. You can become a student of their industry so that you can talk about issues affecting them and their place in the market.

Get to know who the decision makers are. If you want a job with a company, you'll want to know who your boss is going to be. You should also probably know who your co-workers will be and who your boss's boss is going to be too. If you're doing your homework in learning about the company, some of those names will be popping up in articles about the company. You might also get to know LinkedIn and how to use it to find names, connections and networks.

Learn the culture, the language and become familiar. The most important attribute you can build is Trust. Show that you know them, that you want to work for them and with them.

By showing that you want to be a part of the team, that you only want to add value and that you want to help them achieve their objectives, you position yourself as not a salesperson but someone who wants to work for them.

Do the work and become a team player. On your client's team. You'll become indispensable, unstoppable and unshoppable.

CHAPTER 49
GET REAL

How do you make yourself matter to your customers? How did selling today become such a "soft" touch? How did things like liking, loving, trust and mission become more important than prospecting, qualifying, features and benefits and closing, closing, closing?

The reality is that people *usually* buy from people they like. What is *always* true is that people do not buy from people they don't like. So, your job is to be likeable. To be likeable, you need to be authentic, real and willing to risk being yourself.

The number one most important thing you can do is to determine your purpose. I don't mean making money. It needs to be more than that. What drives you? Why do you get up in the morning? What is your purpose behind what you do? If you don't know it, get with someone and work on it. My purpose is to challenge and inspire people so that we can discover our full potential. Now that I know my purpose, decisions around opportunities become a lot easier to make.

When you know your purpose and mission, get very clear about your vision of who are becoming and how you're going to get there. Then share your mission, your vision and your passion with enthusiasm. Let it become your core identity and live it. Be consistent with yourself and make sure you walk your own talk. Never be phony. It will kill your brand.

Be willing to share your unique personality through your voice. But you need to make your voice heard. If you can write—start a blog and do it consistently. If you can speak, get out there and speak. Record videos or podcasts. Share advice and information. Be generous with content and soon people will be listening, watching, asking, sharing and advocating.

If you are a student of your industry and a student of your clients' challenges, you create value. But it's only value if you share it—widely and generously. One of my mentors was PPAI Hall of Fame member, the late, great Glen Holt. Glen never charged me a cent for years of great advice, council and valuable consultations that were a major influence on my career. The biggest gift he gave me though was his example which I try to emulate.

Live out your values and let it show. Only make promises that you KNOW you can keep. Be brave enough to be yourself and share your knowledge. Champion causes outside of your company and yourself and show your charitable nature. Get real and attract your vision and live out your mission.

CHAPTER 50
KNOW YOUR CUSTOMER

How well do you know your customers' business?
Your job is to solve your customers' problems. Period. That's all. You need to become a part of their organization. A vital part if you want to earn the right to charge a little more and be compensated for your expertise.

Think of your job as earning a job at your target prospect's company. This means doing a lot of research. You need to learn not just what they buy, but WHY they buy. What problems are they trying to solve? What is going on in their industry, in their market? You come to this knowledge through observation. You look at their situation. You understand their problems by listening. You ask knowledge-based questions and then listen for their answers. You listen more and talk less.

In the olden days (a couple of years ago), sales trainers used to love to preach "ABC"—Always Be Closing. I contend that the opposite is true. Closing too fast is a quick way out the door. You need to research, listen and then provide feedback on your observations. You need to earn trust by focusing on solving problems.

Help your customer write a success story. The person that you are hoping will hire you to be their branded merchandise consultant is someone you need to get to know so you can help write that story. What does she do every day? What does it take to do their job? What are the problems they face? What frustrates her most?

When you have thought through those questions, you can start to write their story and now it's time to introduce the hero. You. You and your products, services, company and unique creativity. Put on your cape and write the hero's story. About how you can solve their problems and the difference you can make in their lives. Tell the story of the successes you can deliver.

When you provide well-thought-out solutions to your customers' problems, you get the job. You develop a trust-based relationship. You earn loyalty and a higher price.

"...you can start to write their story and now it's time to introduce the hero".

SUMMIT
REACHING THE PEAK OF YOUR POTENTIAL

Part 6: How to Climb to the Summit

- **51** CHAPTER 51: WISHING AND HOPING WILL NOT TAKE YOU TO THE SUMMIT
- **52** CHAPTER 52: BUILD UP THE BASICS
- **53** CHAPTER 53: CHOOSE YOUR MOUNTAIN
- CHAPTER 54: CHOOSE YOUR ROUTE
- **SPEED LIMIT 55** CHAPTER 55: FIND YOUR COMMUNITY
- **56** CHAPTER 56: GET A GOOD GUIDE
- **57** CHAPTER 57: HAVE THE RIGHT GEAR — AND KNOW HOW TO USE IT!
- **58** CHAPTER 58: PLAN, PLAN, PLAN. AND PLAN SOME MORE.
- **59** CHAPTER 59: IT WON'T BE EASY. DO IT ANYWAY.
- CHAPTER 60: SUCCESS IS A MENTAL GAME.

CHAPTER 51

WISHING AND HOPING WILL NOT TAKE YOU TO THE SUMMIT

AFTER MAKING IT to High Camp, 14,000 feet above sea level, on Mt Ararat in eastern Turkey after four days of intense hiking and climbing, I spent summit day alone in my tent. Just a single porter/cook was in the camp to watch over thing. I was left to myself. To go into a full-scale rant of negative self-talk and second thoughts about my failure to summit.

It's amazing how we allow ourselves to talk in a way that we would not accept from others. Internally, I was obsessed—"you loser", "chicken", "DNF—Did Not Finish" and on and on. How could I have given up, folded, just a few hundred yards from camp. I had been reporting my progress up that mountain on social media and had hundreds of people following my adventure. How could I tell them that I failed? I had spent the better part of a week with a group of climbers who would be watching the sun rise from the summit, but I would not be there.

When I got back to the tent, I removed the alpine boots and tried to settle in and go back to sleep but my ego was torturing me. Until I made a decision to change my thinking, I would not be able to own the failure experience, take the lessons and get moving again.

In this defining moment, I started counting the blessing of the moment. I was watching the sun rise on one of the most famous mountains in the world. It was the first mountain I had ever learned about—in Sunday School and the story of Noah's Ark. From my spot outside my tent, I could see Kurdish Turkey, Iran and Armenia. At sixty years old, I had just climbed a mountain to over 14,000 feet—and this was my first mountain at that! After a few years of personal setbacks, I was approaching my second wedding anniversary with April, learning new sports, trying new adventures and enjoying good health. I had no right to be negative. I was experiencing something that few people in the world ever experience.

Seeing the shadow of the mountain created by the sunrise on Summit Day.

Taking ownership of the failure to reach the summit and finding the blessings that it contained brought me to the lessons. My weight was getting in my way. I was pushing over two hundred sixty-five pounds up a mountain with a full pack on my back. I wasn't fit. I hadn't trained for this the way I had trained for marathons in the past. In fact, I had ignored April's advice to learn how to put on crampons or how to use an ice axe. My lack of fitness showed as I was the slowest climber in our group and had less and less confidence each day of the climb.

On that "should have been" Summit Day, I decided to get healthy, flexible and improve my balance. I changed my diet and lost forty-five pounds and made fitness a daily routine. After that experience, I signed up to climb Mt Kilimanjaro—the highest peak on the continent of Africa—19,341 feet above sea level. On July 24, 2014, I reached that summit. Wishing and hoping was not what got me there.

For you to reach the summit—the peak of your potential—apply the practices you would need to take to reach the summit of your mountains.

CHAPTER 52
BUILD UP THE BASICS

IF YOU WANT to reach the summit and be the very best you can be, you need to take care of the basics first. Think about it. In any area of endeavor, those who master the basics will master the game. No team or individual will ever excel without mastery of the basics.

In mountain climbing, this means working on your endurance, your ability to walk long distances and to climb steep angles. You want to be able to walk on uneven ground and keep your balance on sliding rocks and scree, the small loose stones that form a slope on a mountain.

For the promotional professional, it means being an avid student of the profession. You need to master the ability to find sources of products and the ability to use those products to solve a variety of problems. You need to become grounded in sales promotion strategy and tactics, in rewards and recognition and program management.

Use the multitude of educational opportunities that this business has to offer. Attend the educational sessions at trade shows, take the time to participate in webinars and listen to podcasts. Become a reader and consume the trade publications and industry books. Set some personal goals for certification. Take a course on product safety and compliance.

By building up the basics, you'll soon set yourself up as an expert. It is often stated that the promotional products business has a low barrier of entry. Yet, this is a very complex business in which you can never stop learning.

In climbing, one of the basics would be to get in shape. I tried dragging 270 lbs up a mountain with predictable results. In business and in life. Take care of the basics first.

One of the basics is having a business plan. You can move to the head of the class just by fulfilling this BASIC. Industry studies have reported that fewer than 80% of distributors take the time to create a business plan. Go back to Chapter 6 and work on the five questions outlined. When you are done, you will have clear map of what you need to do every step of the way to the top of your mountain.

The basics mean having success habits like prospecting Always and All Ways! You develop your curiosity about who you want to work with and what you have to learn to build relationships with them. You develop consistency of doing the right things in the right way at the right time and then repeat.

Your basics include strengthening your endurance. Your ability to withstand the many disappointments, rejections and incompetence of others that life will throw at you. You know that the win goes to those who won't quit. When things go wrong, you keep going, knowing that your attitude is your secret competitive advantage.

CHAPTER 53
CHOOSE YOUR MOUNTAIN

THE ULTIMATE PEAK is the world's tallest—the highest point on the planet—Mt Everest. At 29,032, it has captured the imagination of adventurers for more than a century. After World War I, it became a matter of national pride to have the first ascent and expeditions of climbers from England, Germany and Switzerland competed for that bragging right.

George Mallory was an Englishman and one of the most experienced climbers of his day. He became consumed with the desire to conquer Everest. In 1921, he made his first attempt and failed. On his second attempt, he not only failed but tragically watched seven of his porters die in an avalanche. It did not diminish his resolve. In 1923, a *New York Times* reporter asked him why he needed to summit Everest. His most famous immortal words were, "Because it's there."

In 1924, he returned for his third attempt. If you're waiting for the happy ending, I'm sorry to disappoint. The first successful ascent was not until May 29, 1953 by Edmund Hillary. Mallory's body was found on the mountain in 1999. Today, about eight hundred people attempt Everest every year. About two-thirds will reach the summit and about one percent will die trying. The cost to make a supported climb will range from $28,000 to $115.000 plus travel and equipment.

My point is not to discourage you from reaching for the highest summit. The point is to summit your mountains. Choose them wisely. Choose the mountains that will bring you joy, happiness and fulfillment. Back to my mountaineering experience, Mt Ararat was a mountain that intrigued me. From my earliest memories, I was told the story of Noah's Ark and of it coming to rest "in the mountains of Ararat." I loved the chance to visit Istanbul and travel to eastern Turkey. The adventure took us to places where the apostle Paul had established first century churches. On the trek up the mountain, we saw nomadic peoples and young shepherds tending their flocks and living much the same way as they did over two thousand years ago.

Mount Ararat the mountain I chose for my first summit attempt.

But importantly, Mt Ararat was an achievable goal. It did not require technical climbing skills. While snow-capped, it was not known for having deadly crevasses or rope assisted climbs.

Choose your mountain and make sure it pushes you to your peak potential. Reach for your highest summit. How can you be the best version of yourself? Make sure you grasp all that is within your reach. But make sure you are making a stretch when you reach!

This all comes back to planning and spending thinking time. If you want to climb a mountain, you will want one that matches your current ability and your aspirations too.

After Ararat, I set my sights on Mt Kilimanjaro. The highest peak in Africa is more famous and is three thousand feet taller than Ararat. But it would not require me to learn to become a technical climber. Like Ararat, it is a snow-capped and dormant volcano and would require planning, preparation and training to acquire the summit.

Make your mountain worthy of you. One that others will look up to. One that makes you proud. Choose your mountain can also be phrased as," What Are You Building?"

Get very clear about what you want from this life. You're creating your

Vision. You're making it real. Why do you want to reach the summit—the peak of your potential? In the words of George Mallory, "Because it's there."

It's there inside of you waiting for you to find it. Go out and enjoy the adventure.

CHAPTER 54
CHOOSE YOUR ROUTE

When deciding to summit one of the great mountains in the world, a climber must decide which route to take. There are seven established routes to climb Mt Kilimanjaro. Each one has certain advantages and disadvantages and different rates of climber success. Each route has varying degrees of difficulty, traffic and quality of the scenery.

The adventurer must also decide how many days of climbing to reach the summit. The more time one allows, the higher their rate of success.

To reach your personal summit and the peak of your potential, you must also choose your route. Like a climber, you'll want to choose the route that will bring you the highest chances of success, the least amount of difficulty and the best scenery along the way.

For some, this may be the road less traveled and a less crowded experience. For others, you may enjoy the company of like-minded adventure seekers like yourself.

Choose your route to your full potential. Your route is your own. So, own it. Another way of thinking about your route is asking yourself, "How will I get there?" or "How will I build my life, business or dreams?" We're talking about your Strategies.

Taking care of your body by making healthy eating and lifestyle habits is a good strategy to make sure you can reach the summit of your potential. It gives you the longevity you need to complete the journey and the vehicle to enjoy it every step of the way. Eating healthy, getting enough sleep, making sure you are exercising while avoiding those things that can kill you.

Practice self-care for a healthy mind. Start each day with gratitude and make it a practice. You'll be amazed how it can pay results in improved creativity and mindfulness. Learn to stop worry in its tracks. Worry is a waste of time and energy. Worry is crazy. That's right. Crazy! Worry is living in the future and there is nothing real about it. Plan—yes. Worry—no.

Go ahead and be selfish and do something that makes you happy. Turn off negative people.

Be your own best friend and tell yourself how awesome you are. Look for beauty and appreciate it. Do something nice for someone. It will boost YOUR spirits. Connect with a friend. Send a thank you note to someone. Every day. Practice your spirituality. No matter what it is. Connect to others and to yourself.

In your business, decide your route. Begin by knowing what you do and more importantly what you do NOT do. Find your niche. Create your uniqueness. Become a specialist. Commit to learning the new skills needed in a changing world. Choose your Target accounts. Know what success looks like. Engage more personally and more frequently with your key stakeholders.

CHAPTER 55
FIND YOUR COMMUNITY

YOU DON'T NEED to climb your mountain alone. In your journey to the peak of your potential and living your best life, develop relationships with like-minded people who share your values, your passions and your commitment to excellence.

You may find them in your faith community. Local networking organizations can be a place to find positive people as well. Just make sure that you find people who are there to give and share and are truly invested in helping you and others reach their summits.

Too many of these networking groups are just about making sales. If you've read this far, you know my belief about that. In my experience, sales have been a result of caring, of providing solutions and of giving first.

You can find them in your regional association. The people committed to certification and lifelong learning are people who are committed to growth and the types of people you will want to learn from and grow with. Most of my oldest, longest lasting friendships and relationships have come from volunteering and participating in industry groups. Joining an association and sitting on the sideline deprives you of the biggest benefit you can derive from membership. Coupon books and discounts may cover the cost of dues, but if you want to really get the best return on your investment—get involved. When you volunteer, you meet other people who are on the journey to make their life the best it can be and working to become the leaders that they can become.

When I was a new member of the National Speakers Association, I went to their national convention. In one of the breakout sessions, the guy sitting next to me asked if I would like to join a Mastermind Group. We soon became friends with three others at various steps in their pursuit of improving as speakers. We had a monthly conference call connecting five people with shared goals who could tell each other which paths led up the mountain and which were the dead ends. Was it comfortable at first to open myself up to four strangers? Heck no. Was it worth it? It was the most valuable thing that I took away from an expensive conference.

There are some good online industry groups where people share their journeys. Some have become outlets for criticism of others, complaining or product searching. Those can be a major waste of your time. Seek out those who want to climb to the peak of their potential and start your own group if you must. Make it private and by invitation only to the people you meet who share your vision and values and dreams.

There is no reason for you to take the journey alone. But it is far worse to have the wrong people in your expedition. Negative people will slow you down. Others will distract you from your ultimate goals. The right people will help you get to where you want to be. The wrong people will take off your path.

CHAPTER 56
GET A GOOD GUIDE

If you were to decide to climb one of the highest mountains in the world, getting the right guide could literally make a difference between not only success and failure, but between life and death.

What do all of the greatest athletes, artists, performers across all industries have in common? They all have a coach. The word "coach" has its origins in transportation—a conveyance to take you from where you are to where you want to go. That's exactly what a good coach can do together with you. Einstein famously defined insanity as doing the same thing over and over again and expecting a different result. If you are stuck, sliding backwards, or moving forward just too frustratingly slowly, it may be time to find a coach to mentor you, challenge you and help launch you to the next level.

When my wife, my sister and I were climbing Mt Kilimanjaro our main coach—guide—was Robert. Robert had experience and knowledge of the mountain, the path, the weather and even who else was on the same route as we were. Every day, he used a pulse oximeter to make sure we were getting enough oxygen to continue our ascent.

The evening before the summit over dinner he asked each of us if we wanted to dedicate the summit to someone or something in our life to add meaning to the culmination of a week of climbing.

As we slowly—take a step, take a breath—made our way up into the thin air, he taught us some Swahili—Juu—meaning "to the top" and encouraged us every step of the way.

When at last the sign on the summit announcing Uhuru Peak came into view, Robert celebrated our success with us. Throughout the expedition, we knew that Robert was watching the weather and that he knew our individual strengths and limitations. We were rewarded with a successful summit.

There are ten ways that working with a coach can help you find your personal power and reach the peak of your potential.

1. Check your alignment. One of the first things that a golf coach will do is make sure you are aimed at your target and that your fundamentals are sound. A good coach will make sure that you have balance and are aligned with your purpose and connected with your calling.

2. Check your blindspot. A coach can help you identify and remove some of the barriers that you may have in place that keep you from achieving your goals and realizing your dreams.

3. Check your progress. By having someone to check in with regularly, you have a new level of accountability. We all become adept a lying to ourselves and making excuses to ourselves that would be obvious BS to anyone else. Reporting your accomplishments, initiatives and steps taken to your coach keeps you focused and on the path to superior results.

4. Life Enrichment. There's more to life than work. A good coach can help you understand a life plan, reduce stress in your life, build a fulfilling balance in your life, improve your relationships with others, improve your self awareness and consciousness, improve your self-discipline and motivation and even improve your health, well-being and happiness.

5. Create your vision. Your coach can assist you in understanding your strengths and how to play to them. You have someone who can help you get very clear about who you are, what your core values are, what you are passionate about and what will provide you with greater abundance in your life.

6. Celebration and Encouragement. Your coach will celebrate your accomplishments and steps toward your personal definition of your summit. There will be times when you need support, nurturing and a source of energy to help you believe in yourself and achieve your dreams. A good coach can help you turn setbacks into comebacks.

7. Raising the bar. Constructive challenge and stretch goals can move you quickly to higher levels of achievement and prosperity. A good coach can identify new skills that you may need and provide you with the resources and options you will need to increase your professional value.

8. Collaborator and co-conspirator. Imagine how much more confident you can be in your new ideas, creativity and innovation when you've bounced them off a practiced, experienced professional who has worked through the challenges that you are now facing. Your coach is a sounding board and a veteran who can show you the short cuts learned through experience.

9. Non-judgmental. Tell your coach anything. The things you wouldn't share with anyone else are safe with a good coach. A good coach is trained to be non-judgmental and objective. They will show you where your thoughts are not congruent with your goals or your values. They will share where and if they have seen ideas work or fall short. Try out any thought or idea and together discover what is brilliant and what to discard.

10. Playing the bounce. Change comes at us fast. Life brings surprises, set-backs, changing circumstances and economic realities. Technology is a game changer at every turn. Your coach can help you step back and see the big picture and how it is affecting your industry and your clients. Your coach can help you prepare, adjust and bounce back.

Don't start climbing into the unknown without a guide. Find the right one and have a partner in your success.

CHAPTER 57
HAVE THE RIGHT GEAR – AND KNOW HOW TO USE IT!

Reaching High Camp on Mt Ararat, I put on my alpine climbing boots, attached brand new crampons and grabbed a beautiful Black Diamond Ice Axe. They did not get me to the summit. Because, that afternoon when we reached High Camp and the base of the glacier that covers the top of the mountain was the very first time I wore the boots, attached the crampons or handled the ice axe. Heck, the ice axe could have been a screwdriver or a crowbar for all the good it would have done me had I fallen on the ice and started sliding down the mountain.

When I stepped out onto the glacier to "practice" climbing in alpine boots and crampons, I lasted about fifteen minutes before my left crampon was falling off the boot at odd angles. Although an experienced climber in our expedition rigged them up for me, that equipment failure and the echoing voice in my head of my wife's suggestions (some call it nagging, she calls it motivational speaking) that I get out and work with the equipment in Michigan snow and ice at seven hundred feet above sea level instead of on the side of a mountain fifteen thousand feet above sea level were a huge reason why I turned around on summit morning and pouted and felt sorry for myself instead of having a triumphant summit.

If you want to become the best professional, you can be and reach your full potential you will need to have the right tools and learn how to use them. You will need to embrace change. Don't just accept change. Your customers are multi-generational now. You need to learn how to relate to Gen Z, Millennials, Gen Xers and Baby Boomers the way that they want to be contacted.

I used to say, if you hate social media, you're going to suck at social media. But news flash! If you want to reach today's customers, you will need to love social media and get good at it. You still need to go to the customer and that is where they are spending their time.

After the experience on Mt Ararat of not knowing how to use the right gear, I learned. Climbing a glacier in Wrangell-St Elias National Park, Alaska 2016.

You need to learn technology including ways for your customers to enjoy conducting ecommerce with you. Amazon brought about new expectations about the online experience. The pandemic drove late adaptors to learn how to research, compare, customize and buy online. You need to get the tools and learn how to use them well so you can be more relevant to the needs of your customers.

Working from home is the new normal. It's not going to be easy to call on customers in their office now that their office is their bedroom. You need to not just use virtual tools such as Zoom. You need to get good at it. Study it, practice with your lighting and your audio and your backgrounds.

Remember. You need to have the right gear. That may mean some major expense or require affiliating with organizations that have made the investment. But it also means you need to learn how to use those tools. That can be uncomfortable. It can make your head hurt. Do it anyway.

Great equipment will not do you any good if you don't know how to use it. Make sure you have the right gear for your mountain. The gear you need for enterprise (multi-national) accounts is different than small local accounts. But you need to have the gear and the skills to use them so you can reach your summit.

CHAPTER 58
PLAN, PLAN, PLAN. AND PLAN SOME MORE.

YOU WOULD JUST drive to Lone Pine, California and start hiking up Mt Whitney, the highest peak in the lower forty-eight states. To reach the summit of this 14,505-foot peak in the Sierra Nevada range, requires all of the factors described in the previous seven chapters.

You would have to build up the basics of mountain climbing plus learn technical skills beyond those. You would need to make sure you knew a route to the top and will have wanted to spoken with others who have experienced the climb. A good guide and having the right gear and knowing how to use that gear would be critical to both your success and your survival.

All of this requires planning which has been discussed in previous chapters but warrants continuous emphasis. President Dwight D Eisenhower made this paradoxical statement about planning. "Plans are worthless, but planning is everything." In life, in warfare, in business, or even in mountain climbing—you cannot plan for everything. But you need to be ready for anything.

On a mountain, storms can come up quickly or in glacial areas, avalanches can happen and force re-routing. In life, accidents, sickness and the unexpected can happen. In business, new disruptors come into the market, economic downturns occur and even once every hundred years or so an international pandemic may force changes in your plans.

Several years ago, within a matter of months, a close friend who was training me to join his successful consulting business died of a sudden heart attack, the owner of the company I was with committed suicide, my marriage failed, my estranged wife was diagnosed with Stage IV cancer. She died on the day of my mother's funeral. And then the market crashed, and the Great Recession began.

Clearly none of this was planned. To be honest, exactly how to deal with it wasn't planned either. But planning based on a clear vision of what I wanted from life, determination to live out core values that I believed, and taking responsibility for my own thoughts and attitude allowed me to move through a series of events and live with gratitude and a sense of purpose.

Here's the thing. Plan. Have a business plan and a life plan and create a road map that can get you there. If your road gets washed out, remember where you're going and adjust your plan. Be flexible in your strategies and tactics but relentless in your purpose and vision.

Similar to Eisenhower's quote, a British correspondent in "The Daily News back in 1877 remarked, "plans are worthless when the fighting is once begun." So be prepared. Have a plan but allow flexibility in your planning. Know when to zig and when to zag but never forget your final destination.

Albert Einstein once said, "Do not try to become a person of success but try to become a person of value." When you measure your success by how far you come while staying true to who you are and who you wish to become, you will discover success. You will discover the peak of your potential. You will reach your summit.

CHAPTER 59
IT WON'T BE EASY. DO IT ANYWAY.

It was on Day 4 of our trek to summit Mt Kilimanjaro when we reached the Barranco Wall. The rocky vertical rock face is 843 feet tall made up of steep narrow paths cut back and forth making it a class 4 scramble. That means you don't need technical equipment or skills, but you do need to use all four of your limbs to get over it. It takes about an hour to two hours of scrambling to make this passage. We were about two thirds of the way up the wall when my sister, a veteran of fifty marathons including the Boston Marathon, muttered "Marathons are for wimps!"

Our assistant guide, George leads us up and over the Barranco Wall on Mt Kilimanjaro

My first marathon was the Columbus (OH) marathon which I ran about a year after first celebrating being able to run non-stop from one telephone pole to the next. About the time I got to Mile 20, it felt like my feet were just crushed. Every footfall hurt. Eventually, I saw Mile 25 and was overcome with emotion. I had 1.2 miles to go but at that point I knew that I would make to the finish line. I didn't know if I would be running, walking, crawling or dragging my body—but I knew I would make it.

My experience is that the good stuff happens at the edge or just off the edge of our comfort zone. You will experience things that will tempt you into quitting. Things will make you question your sanity. "Why am I doing this?" But then you do it and the feeling of accomplishment makes you forget the pains on the journey.

Commitment will get you through the tough spots. Jim Rohn said, "Motivation is what gets you started. Commitment is what keeps you going." Personally, I've always liked Winston Churchill's advice, "When you're going thru Hell, keep on going!"

There is no joy or satisfaction in living small. You will never know how far you can go until you just keep on keeping on. Over my career I had the privilege of working with some huge accounts. Yeah, little ol' me, college dropout from Kalamazoo, MI son of a brick mason. Accounts like Kellogg's, Whirlpool, Wolverine Worldwide and Elmer's Glue happened because they were goals that I pursued. I never doubted that I could handle them or land them. But I landed them because I never gave up. In one case, it took nineteen years, but it happened.

Believe in yourself and your ideas and never give up. My biggest projects often had to be sold, revised, sold again and repeat. But I learned to never accept a "no" from someone who didn't have the authority to say "yes". Reaching your peak potential means you have chosen your mountain and have the confidence in your ability to reach for the top.

The principle of "doing it anyway, even when it's hard" gives you feeling of accomplishment that is hard to describe. You have the satisfaction of knowing that when others quit, you kept on keeping on.

CHAPTER 60
SUCCESS IS A MENTAL GAME

Know that you can reach the peak of your potential. Sports are a great analogy for pursuing excellence in all areas of our life. Athletic success and subsequently life success often hinges upon work ethic, competitiveness, self-control, perseverance, focus and mental strength.

One needs the willingness to do the work to get the results. This means having the drive to push yourself to be more and to achieve more. Competitiveness is a hunger to win and the absolute refusal to be satisfied with "good enough". Great performance comes from a passion for achieving personal bests and personal improvement. In my twenty marathons, I never came close to a top ten finish. (Unless there were only ten people in my age group—then I had a chance). At the Bermuda marathon my motivation was to get to the water stations before they took them down. One year at the Chicago Marathon it took me fourteen miles to pass a man on crutches! But in all of those races, I started and finished ahead of every person who didn't start.

Top performers learn the importance of self-control of maintaining composure and remaining calm even when things don't turn out the way they should. One time I rightfully corrected a brand manager client whose actions and my misunderstanding of his intent made me feel mightily self-righteous. Oh, I was so right and so wrong. Had I focused on the relationship and the long-term goal, I likely would have landed the account where he went to work next. Instead, I had a reverse two-fer. I lost his current and future business.

Perseverance is a theme covered many times in this book. I truly believe perseverance or call it resilience is the key for all of us to reach our summits. Approach your goals and your vision and challenges with a steadfast attitude. Set your mind to your goals and do not stop until you achieve it. Get knocked down. Get back up. You never fail until you quit short of your goal.

Get a laser-focus on what you want. Like an athlete, get into the "zone" and concentrate on your vision. Know what is important and stay on task. Take a break from email, social media or whatever your distractions are that take your eyes off your prize.

Mental strength is what will get you to the summit to the peak of your potential and your best version of yourself. Mental toughness will put you back on your path. You alone have full control of your attitude, your self-talk, and the choices that will bring you the life you deserve. It is the key to managing your emotions. It is what will give you the attributes we discussed. It will push you to persevere. It will silence your self-doubt. It will give you the courage to start, to fail and to start again. It will push you through your discomfort zones and give you courage. It will help you ignore the naysayers and negative garbage thinkers who would love to see you be as mediocre as they are. It will give the wisdom to analyze and learn from your mistakes. Mental strength will give you the power to bounce back from setbacks and keep on climbing.

ABOUT
THE AUTHOR

PAUL A KIEWIET has spent a career building brands. He founded a sales promotion agency in 1982 and worked with some of America's most beloved brands including Elmer's Glue, Krylon Spray Paints, Kellogg's, Coca Cola, Whirlpool, Kitchen Aid, Borden, Hush Puppies, Rocky Shoes and Boots, Wyler's, Soup Starter, RainDance, Kroger, DowBrands, Tobler-Suchard, Mentos and many more. He was active in the point of purchase, premium incentive and promotional products industries. Paul served on the board of directors of the Promotional Products Association International and was chairman of the board of directors in 2007-2008.

He is a Certified Incentive Professional, Master Advertising Specialist Plus, and Certified Life Coach. Kiewiet was inducted into the Michigan Promotional Professionals Hall of Fame in 2010 and into the Promotional Products Association International Hall of Fame in 2015. A frequent and popular speaker and educator, industry consultant and coach he authored the chapter on promotional products in Enterprise Engagement—The Textbook. His magazine articles were recognized with the EXCEL Award from the Society of Non-Profit Association Publications and the prestigious FOLIO award. Kiewiet has been honored for creativity and results with fourteen Pyramid Awards from PPAI, two ASI Spirit Awards including Marketer of the Year. Kiewiet has also won the President's Award from the National Premium Sales Executives and a Golden Key Award from the Incentive Manufacturers Association.

He has reached millions of marketing professionals emphasizing the importance of connecting with important values in order to create value in the marketplace. From Bogotá to Beijing, Dusseldorf and to hundreds of audiences around the country, Kiewiet is in high demand as a speaker, coach and consultant. His articles have appeared in numerous business publications and podcasts of his presentations have been featured on CBS Radio, the American Marketing Association, and on USAirways Sky Radio. He has been quoted in Fortune, Forbes, The Wall Street Journal, The New York Times, B2B Magazine, Kiplinger Newsletter and Wired magazine.

He has been trained in Gallup University on positive emotions and Marcus Buckingham-trained for strength-based alignment. He has served as a trustee, board member and/or officer of the Forum for People Performance Management and Measurement at Northwestern University, National Premium Sales Executives, and the Association of Incentive Marketing. In addition to speaking, writing, coaching and consulting, he is the Executive Director of the Michigan Promotional Professionals Association.

Paul lives in Grand Rapids, MI and enjoys biking, hiking, pickleball, fishing, stand-up paddleboard, skiing, music, arts and Lake Michigan. He loves to travel and explore and has been to six of the seven continents—only Antarctica remains on his bucket list. He has completed twenty 26.2-mile marathons, climbed 103 stories to the top of Willis Tower and survived a Warrior Dash. He and his wife have stand up paddle boarded the five Great Lakes, annually run the 8-mile Mackinac Island Run, went diving in the Great Barrier Reef and climbed Mt. Ararat. They summited Mt. Kilimanjaro and traveled the world. In 2019, he and his wife and mother-in-law walked up the entire state of Michigan from Indiana to Canada.

Paul believes that when you connect people with their higher purpose you can drive them to amazing performances and prosperity. His "why?" is to inspire and challenge people so that we can realize our full potential.

Paul can be reached at create2bgreat@gmail.com. You may share your journey at www.summit-book.com.

On the summit of Mt Kilimanjaro, the highest peak on the continent of Africa at 19,341' above sea level.

Made in the USA
Columbia, SC
22 December 2021